# WEB
# SERVICES
## *EXPLAINED*

## Solutions and Applications for the Real World

ISBN 0-13-047963-2

90000

9 780130 479631

# WEB SERVICES EXPLAINED

## Solutions and Applications for the Real World

Joe Clabby

PRENTICE HALL PTR
UPPER SADDLE RIVER, NJ 07458
WWW.PHPTR.COM

**Library of Congress Cataloging-in-Publication Data**

Clabby, Joe.
  Web services explained : solutions and applications for the real world / Joe Clabby.
    p. cm.
  Includes index.
  ISBN 0-13-047963-2
    1. Web site development. 2. Application software--Development. 3. Web
  sites--Standards. I. Title.

  TK5105.888 .C543 2002
  005.2'76--dc21                                    2002070353


Editorial/production supervision: *Laura Burgess*
Composition: *MetroVoice Publishing Services*
Cover design director: *Jerry Votta*
Cover design: *Talar Boorujy*
Art director: *Gail Cocker-Bogusz*
Manufacturing buyer: *Maura Zaldivar*
Senior managing editor: *Karen McLean*
Editorial assistant: *Richard Winkler*
Marketing manager: *Bryan Gambrel*

Prentice Hall books are widely used by corporations and government agencies for training, marketing, and resale.

For information regarding corporate and government bulk discounts please contact:
Corporate and Government Sales (800) 382-3419 or corpsales@pearsontechgroup.com

IBM, MQSeries, PowerPC, OS/400, SAA, WebSphere, and VisualAge are all trademarks or registered trademarks of IBM Corporation; OMG and CORBA are trademarks or registered trademarks of OMG; Microsoft, BizTalk, Windows, Microsoft SQL Server and Visual Studio are trademarks or registered trademarks of Microsoft; SUN, Java, Solaris, and iPlanet are trademarks or registered trademarks of Sun Microsystems Inc. in the United States and other countries; Intel is a registered trademark of Intel Corporation; BEA and WebLogic are registered trademarks of BEA Systems; Compaq is a registered trademark of Compaq Computer Corporation; Oracle is a registered trademark of Oracle Corporation; Sabre is a registered trademark of Sabre; SAP and mySAP.com are registered trademarks of SAP AG in Germany and in several other countries all over the world; UNIX is a registered trademark of The Open Group; PeopleSoft is a registered trademark of PeopleSoft; InterPro is a registered trademark of InterPro; mhe.net and SecureCreditServer are trademarks or registered trademarks of mhe.net, Inc.; Bluestone is a registered trademark of Hewlett-Packard; IONA and ORBIX E2A are trademarks or registered trademarks of IONA; Borland, Delphi, C++Builder and Jbuilder are all trademarks or registered trademarks of Borland Software Corp.; Jasmine is a registered trademark of Computer Associates International Inc.; Macromedia and ColdFusion are registered trademarks of Macromedia, Inc.; CodeWarrior is a registered trademark of Metrowerks; PETRODEX is a trademark of GE Information Services. All other company and product names mentioned herein are the trademarks or registered trademarks of their respective owners.

Printed in the United States of America

10   9   8   7   6   5   4   3   2   1

ISBN 0-13-047963-2

Pearson Education LTD.
Pearson Education Australia PTY, Limited
Pearson Education Singapore, Pte. Ltd.
Pearson Education North Asia Ltd.
Pearson Education Canada, Ltd.
Pearson Educación de Mexico, S.A. de C.V.
Pearson Education—Japan
Pearson Education Malaysia, Pte. Ltd.

# Contents

# Summary Observations and Conclusions   197

# Preface

If you are a nontechnical business executive and you rely on computer-based information systems for doing your job, you must learn about Web services. Web services are a newly evolving set of distributed application development standards that enable applications to easily cooperate and share information and data with other applications. These evolving standards are expected to radically alter the ways in which applications are built and deployed, information is presented and shared, and software is bought and sold.

Enterprises that adopt Web services will be able to react more quickly and nimbly to changing market conditions. They will be able to take advantage of new efficiencies in business process flow that will serve to lower their sales, general, and administrative costs. They will be able to broaden the application services that they offer to their customers and business partners. And they will be able to use Web services to help them penetrate new markets.

Web services will fundamentally change the business models that underlie many successful businesses today. Failure to prepare for this change will leave many organizations at a competitive disadvantage in the long term. To ensure your organization's longevity, you need to learn what Web services are, what they can do for your organization, how they work, how they can be used, and how your organization can go about building a Web services information infrastructure.

## Approach

This book is structured to provide 10 answers that business executives are likely to seek as they investigate Web services. Each chapter considers a basic question, such as

"What are Web services?" Key topics to be discussed—highlights—are listed at the beginning of each chapter. The chapter then provides information and analysis on these topics, concluding with a summary of what the reader should have learned.

The 10 questions this book closely considers are:

1. What are Web services?
2. What are program-to-program communications?
3. How do specific Web services technologies actually work?
4. Where are the limitations, shortcomings, and "gotchas" of this architecture?
5. What can these technologies enable my organization to do?
6. Who is using Web services now (and in what ways)?
7. When should my organization adopt Web services?
8. What vendor selection criteria should be used?
9. Which approach should my organization use—.NET or J2EE?
10. How should my organization compare, contrast, and differentiate the product and service offerings of various Web services vendors?

An appendix section presents profiles of various randomly chosen vendors. These provide an overview of offerings by prospective vendor partners that provide Web services solutions.

## Focus

Dozens upon dozens of new books are available on the topic of "Web services." Here are some reasons for choosing to read this one:

- **Nontechnical approach**: This book is thoroughly nontechnical. It provides the necessary basic familiarization with certain technical concepts such as program-to-program communications, registries (directories), and "protocols," but its main focus is on the strategic business benefits that can be derived from Web services.

- **Learning by example**: This book uses theoretical as well as real-world scenarios to illustrate what is strategically possible as well as what is being accomplished using Web services. It shows how Web services can be and are being used to create competitive advantage, to modify product packaging, to reduce development costs, and the like. The theoretical examples show business executives how they can potentially exploit Web services; the real-world examples show them what is being done using Web services today.

- **Determining vendor selection criteria**: This book also helps business executives determine the right selection/buying criteria for their respective organizations to use in accessing Web services products and services. It describes three approaches that can be used to create or obtain Web services applications, and it gives examples of vendor offerings using each approach. This analysis should help business executives more quickly determine the approach they will use and the vendor(s) they may choose in order to rapidly implement Web services application solutions within their enterprises.

These foci make this book:

- a *primer* on Web services;
- an *idea/strategic planning guide*; and
- a *buyer's guide*.

If you are seeking to find out what Web services are, how to use them, and which type of vendor to partner with or to buy Web services products from, then this book is for you!

## Getting the Most Out of This Book

This is not one of those entertaining quick-read business books. It provides a tremendous amount of research material as well as analysis, saving you hundreds of hours of doing your own fundamental Web services research and analysis. It crosses several disciplines (technology, business strategy, vendor criteria and selection, and more)—it's a challenging read.

To meet this challenge you'll need to "get psyched" about Web services! You'll need to remind yourself, "I have to know this material to ensure the long-range success of my company." You'll need to look for the gleam of excitement in "application development environments" and "program-to-program" communications.

Further, for maximum learning benefit, do not try to read this book "all in one sitting." Treat each chapter as a mini-white paper. Read it, then put the book down and walk away from it. Come back when you've had a chance to consider what you've learned. This approach will help you maximize your learning experience while keeping your interest high.

Also, take the opportunity to access the Internet source sites referred to in each chapter. More in-depth information on each topic can be gleaned by visiting these sources.

## The Importance of Perseverance

If the preceding section has piqued your interest in Web services—read on. But be forewarned: Web services are a new, Web standards-based way to develop distributed, shared applications across disparate computer systems environments over the Internet. Accordingly, Web services discussions are really about "application development environments"—a challenging topic that calls upon your perseverance in assimilating it.

For those who persevere and learn the basics of the "Web services" approach/business model, the potential rewards of using it are substantial. You can expect a direct and positive effect in terms of lowering business/transaction costs and application development costs, improving your company's time-to-market in delivering software solutions to your customers and business partners, sharpening your response to competitive pressure, and improving overall business efficiency. Understanding the Web services model can also help your business to take competitive advantage as well as open new sources of revenue by remarketing existing applications.

Understanding the answers to the 10 questions considered in this book will enable business executives to (a) define Web services, (b) extrapolate where Web services fit within their respective organizations, (c) determine how and when to exploit Web services for their organization's strategic and competitive advantage, and (d) understand the criteria for selecting which vendors' products and services should be used to move their enterprises into the Web services world.

*So, in other words, please stick with it—the time you invest will be rewarded, you will save hundreds of hours of research and analysis, and you will pick up very valuable strategic and competitive information while learning about the evolving world of Web services.*

# Executive Summary

A change is underway in the computing industry that is as significant as the initial adoption of the Internet for business use. This change will affect all aspects of the computer industry—the way computer software is made, how it is sold, how it is deployed, and on what it will run. It will affect how small, medium, and large enterprises acquire and build applications; it will affect how independent software vendors (ISVs) build their products and take them to market; it will affect how value-added resellers (VARs) actually "add value" to the systems they sell by integrating applications; it will affect how original equipment manufacturers (OEMs) build computing hardware and infrastructure; and it will also affect how service providers [application solutions providers (ASPs), Internet service providers (ISPs), etc.] deploy software and sell service solutions.

On the enterprise side of the business, this change will affect how companies build and exploit their application portfolios; it will reduce the cost of development for specialized or custom applications; it will make the enterprise more responsive to changing market and competitive conditions; and it will increase workers' productivity.

This change goes right to the heart of how businesses can be structured and operated. It has the potential to fundamentally shift the very models upon which all businesses are built. As a result of the coming together of Web data formats, Web services, and the Internet, a new, very flexible application development model is emerging. This new model will fundamentally alter the way that enterprises, VARs, OEMs, ISVs, and service providers conduct their respective businesses.

## What Is This Change?

What we are talking about is a way of enabling applications to work transparently and cooperatively with each other across diverse computer-system/platform/operating-system/language environments. It is both a concept and a suite of Internet standards designed to enable Web-based program-to-program communications. We call it *Web services*.

The leader in bringing about this standardization is the World Wide Web Consortium, also known as the W3C. This organization consists of 60-plus researchers and engineers and *over 500 member organizations* (as well as individual contributors) who are helping to create Web standards for interoperability, access, semantics, trust, evolvability, decentralization, and multimedia. For more information on this standards body visit *www.W3C.org*.

## What Do Web Services Enable Your Organization to Do?

Web services are expected to affect the way in which IT systems are designed, deployed, and purchased.

Business enterprises, instead of having to develop applications internally and house them within direct control of the IT department, will obtain run-the-business applications as service from outside third-party service providers. Your organization, then, will "purchase" software differently (as a service). It will be able to greatly expand its application portfolio without having to build comprehensive applications in the traditional monolithic and centralized manner. This, in turn, will enable your organization to save development time, provide faster time-to-market with new application services for its customers, and respond more quickly to new competitive pressures.

With the additional help of business process management software, your organization can streamline the flow of business internally or with business partners—improving organizational efficiency and lowering the cost of running a business.

Web services can also give your organization a way to remarket existing intellectual content.

These same concepts hold true for ISVs, VARs, and OEMs and systems software makers (as illustrated in Figure 0–1).

In short, Web services will create new efficiencies for all kinds of businesses that rely on information technologies. Web services have the potential to change the very founda-

**Enterprises**
- Reduce development costs
- Faster time-to-market
- Ability to quickly respond to changing market conditions or competitive threats
- Ability to dynamically grow applications portfolio
- Ability to resell existing applications (found money)

**ISVs**
- Reduce development and quality assurance costs
- Ability to quickly respond to changing market conditions or competitive situations
- Ability to create functionally richer products more quickly
- Ability to create new marketing channels
- Ability to package software more creatively to reach new buying audiences

**A New Business Model Made Possible by Newly Evolved Internet "Web Services" Standards**

**VARs**
- Enables VARs to do what VARs should do—add value by integrating applications
- A new source of revenue—Web-based application integration services

**OEMs/System S/W**
- Levels the applications playing field
- New focus on creating the best infrastructure
- True hardware independence

FIGURE 0-1    Web Services: The Changing Business Model.

tion (the business model) upon which many businesses are currently based.

## What Are Web Services?

The quick answer is: Web services are a distributed computing architecture. Only this particular architecture makes use of loosely coupled applications, as opposed to tightly coupled applications, to enable applications to communicate. This tightly coupled concept radically affects how information systems will work in the future—a theme that will be explored in depth in this book.

The longer answer is that Web services pertain to:

1. How data is presented/shared using a content/format approach called "XML"—eXtensible Markup Language. Most information is shared on the Internet today using a language called HTML. HTML is great for displaying (presenting) text and graphics—but XML tells cooperating application programs what the data is (a name, address, phone number, etc.) and thus enables developers to control, display, share, and manipulate data (rather than presenting data graphics and static information).

2. How applications find services and share information and data across diverse systems environments, using Web services registries and templates/interfaces known as:

   - Universal Description, Discovery, and Integration (UDDI)—a "registry standard" that allows applications to be listed and located;

   - WSDL (Web Services Description Language)—a "template" that allows applications to describe to other applications the rules for interfacing and interacting;

   - SOAP (Simple Object Access Protocol)—a programmatic interface that enables applications to bind together and commence program-to-program communications.

3. How communications take place over a common network (the Internet) using HTTP protocol as the transport.

SIDEBAR 0-1
QUICK DEFINITIONS

Protocol—In this book a protocol is a way that applications can "talk" to each other.
Protocols can be established ways to send and receive data over a network, or they
can be tacit agreements between applications on what procedures should be
observed when sharing information (for instance, how one application should respond
to the request of another application for data or information).
Registry—A registry is simply a place where an application program can "register"
characteristics about itself (how to communicate with it, or what it does, etc.). The
word "directory" is often used synonymously with "registry," but directories provide
somewhat different functions, such as user account or configuration information, and
are less often used as repositories for application information characteristics.
It is important to know what protocols are and what they do in order to understand
how Web services are able to share information with other applications on disparate
systems. Further, it is important to understand the "registry" concept because
registries will play a crucial role in helping Web services applications find each other
and work with each other in the future.

"Web services" refers also to what the aforementioned standards *do*—they enable certain applications to provide *computational*, *messaging*, or *transactional services* for other
applications, regardless of the platform, operating system,
or programming language the originating application is
running on.

# But There's More to Web Services Than Just UDDI, WSDL, and SOAP

Many writers limit their discussion of Web services to a
description of the UDDI registry and WSDL/templates/
SOAP programmatic interface. This is fine if you just want
to understand what the formal Web services standards are.

But UDDI registry and WSDL/SOAP are only half of the picture. To understand Web services you need to understand what XML is and what it can do. You also need to understand how application development environments are being tied to Web services to make application development easier. And you need to realize that, for Web services to be used in enterprise-class mission-critical computing environments, issues such as reliability, security, and routing will need to be addressed. To function in real-world production environments Web services need to match the sophistication of more mature architectures such as Common Object Request Broker Architecture or Electronic Data Interchange—which means that additional standards must be developed to deal with complex routing, security, and reliability issues and a whole host of other enterprise-class architectural issues (detailed later in this book). Without these additional improvements, Web services will be merely an "interesting" messaging service.

Further, to truly exploit Web services, attention needs to be paid to application development environments, business process/work flow, and business process management—as well as to information presentation, personalization, and system integration. Over time, standards committees will deal with these issues, but meanwhile, failure to adequately address them will limit the use of Web services in a live enterprise-class environment.

As you will see later in this book, significant changes and improvements are underway that will help make Web services viable for production use in enterprises. You will see that entire architectures growing up around Web services communications protocols and registry services are helping to fill in the gaps until the standards mature. (These architectures are offered by companies like IBM and Microsoft.) You will also find that Web services applications can be built and deployed using XML for information transfer and other protocols and approaches for program-to-program communications. In other words, vendors are adding functionality to compensate for certain Web services shortcomings (like security), while other protocols can be used until Web services protocols and registries mature a bit more.

## What's So Special about Web Services?

Web services can do all of the following:

- *Enable application developers to stop worrying about systems infrastructure and instead focus on writing cooperative applications.* Web services combined with XML enable applications to be written in any of the most popular programming languages and deployed on any of the most popular systems platforms. This makes much of the complexity in writing program-to-program applications (applications that can work cooperatively with each other, usually across systems environments) transparent and thus greatly simplifies the job of applications programmers. (At long last, programmers can focus more on writing useful applications and less on making those applications work with underlying systems infrastructure.)
- *Help cut down on application development time and expense.* (Developers can make use of existing applications modules rather than having to write new service applications from scratch every time they write a new program.)
- *Enable application writers to dynamically grow application portfolios.* (In other words, enable application developers to assemble *compound application solutions* more quickly than ever before using internally created "modules" as well as externally created modules to build compound applications quickly, so that enterprises can bring new products and features to market more expeditiously.)
- *Open new marketing opportunities for enterprises that already have applications.* Existing applications can be sold as Web services modules (providing a potential new source of revenue to the enterprise).
- *Enable enterprises to respond more quickly to changing market conditions* (e.g., new buyer trends) *or to competitive pressures.*
- *Help consumers and business users get access to highly personalized applications* that can run on multiple different devices (PCs, handhelds, smart phones, etc.).

### Nine Reasons to Embrace Web Services Architecture

1. Rapidly open new markets
2. Create new organizational efficiencies
3. Reduce application development costs
4. Create/overcome competitive pressure
5. Create new sources of revenue using existing intellectual capital
6. Repackage existing products to better reach/serve existing markets
7. Solve systems inoperability problems
8. Dynamically grow an existing applications portfolio
9. Increase/improve organizational and individual productivity

**FIGURE 0-2**   Nine Ways to Advantageously Use Web Services.

These are but a few of the benefits offered by the Web services application development and deployment model! Many others relate to using Web services to create new go-to-market approaches and new efficiencies, reduce costs, repackage existing products or intellectual material, and so on. This book focuses on nine of these benefits (see Figure 0–2).

# I've Heard This All Before—Are Web Services for Real?

Information Systems executives have heard vendors and standards organizations pitch program-to-program distributed computing architectures for two decades.

For example, in the early 1980s IBM introduced its Systems Application Architecture (SAA) and a concept called "program-to-program" communications that had aims similar to those of Web services today. IBM had its own format for information transfer, Document Content Architecture (DCA), its own protocol for enabling programs to "speak" to each other: Logical Unit 6.2 [LU6.2—an application program interface (API)]; and its own protocol to bind sessions: peer-to-peer Physical Unit 2.1 (PU 2.1—a peer systems communications protocol).

Apollo had a program-to-program architecture based on Remote Procedure Calls (RPCs); Microsoft had one of its own (Distributed Network Architecture—DNA); the Object Management Group introduced a solution called Common

Object Request Broker Architecture (CORBA); the Open Software Foundation offered DCE, and so on.

Each of these architectures used the same basic approach: a common data format; a common suite of application program interfaces (APIs); and a common network environment. Today's Web services are architected in the same manner—format, APIs, network communications protocols. For instance, IBM's architecture had a common content/format de facto standard (DCA as compared with Web services' XML content/format); a common API (LU 6.2 as compared with communications protocols found in WSDL and SOAP); and a common communications standard (PU 2.1 over an SNA-based protocol network as opposed to today's HTTP and TCP/IP protocols over the Internet).

So, are Web services just another distributed computing scheme? If not, why will Web services succeed where others have failed?

**How Web Services Differ from Previous Architectures**

The fundamental objective in distributed computing is the same now as it was 20 years ago: to enable applications to work cooperatively with other applications over a common network. This time, however, Web services:

- Use fluid, as-needed, loosely coupled connections between applications. This loosely coupled approach means that applications can find each other and automatically request and recieve "services." This approach has very significant advantages (see Figure 0–2) over earlier distributed computing architectures that use a hard-coding method to link applications together.
- Allow for the use of differing programming languages between cooperating programs (rather than requiring that programs all be written in the same language in order to interoperate).
- Allow information to flow more smoothly through corporate networks and through supply chains (XML documents can move freely and securely though security firewalls).
- Make it possible for applications to find each other and work cooperatively together (as opposed to hav-

ing to "hard-code" the locations of cooperating pro-grams in order to enable requester applications to find and work with service applications).

- Have the advantage of one common network (the Internet) as opposed to multiple competing networks (such as SNA, TCP/IP, OSI, IPX/SPX, and other net-work schemes) to enable systems and applications to communicate with each other. Almost every distrib-uted systems and applications vendor supports Inter-net communications.

By being able to find each other, Web services applications can request and obtain transactional, messaging, or computa-tional services—then recede until the service is again required. This fluid and dynamic approach makes Web ser-vices distinctly different from previous attempts to build a ubiquitous program-to-program communications architecture.

## Issues, Shortcomings, Gotchas...

Now for a dose of reality. Web services hold great promise as a means to help businesses improve efficiency and effec-tiveness, but they still have some growing up to do.

On the positive side, the fundamental Web services architec-ture is sound. The standards that have been developed are generally simple to implement and consist of a common means to create content and formats (XML) that can be shared between disparate systems. UDDI is becoming a reg-istry standard; WSDL is adequate for helping applications figure out how to work together; SOAP is useful for enabling applications to talk to each other; and HTTP (a transport protocol) is well known in the industry and makes a good default common protocol.

On the negative side you will find that:

- Few public UDDI directories exist. Hence, getting your Web service "known" will be difficult.
- WSDL needs to be made richer to allow for more auto-mated program-to-program negotiation. For instance,

WSDL needs to include the ability to negotiate payments for services delivered (because this is how many Web services providers will make money).

- More work needs to be done by the standards committees to address messaging reliability, security, routing, and the handling of complex transactions.

In other words, Web services standards need to become more mature, particularly in secure transactional environments where reliability, availability, and performance are key considerations if a system is to be used in mission-critical computing situations.

**Alternatives**     These "gotchas" have been identified to make you aware of current shortcomings of the Web services architecture. Later on, this book discusses some of the standard committee activities that will help remedy them. Meanwhile, be aware that the shortcomings of existing Web services standards do not necessarily prohibit their use for a variety of light-transactional or heavily message-oriented applications where requirements for reliability, security, and manageability may be less stringent than those of mission-critical application environments. Also, it is my position that Web services architecture can be augmented by various third-party hardware and/or software products. In doing so, issues such as security, reliability, transaction handling, performance tuning, and the like can be readily overcome.

There are two ways to "work around" current Web services shortcomings:

1. Use a similar architecture such as CORBA or COM to create Web services type applications (see Figure 0–3); or
2. Augment existing Web services protocols with other products that help fill in the gaps.

Figure 0–3 illustrates how many early adopters are implementing Web services today. In this example the object is to move XML data between two points (on the right and left). If an enterprise has strong requirements for reliability, security, and manageability, other architectures such as EDI and CORBA can be used to move XML data. If an enterprise has a lower priority, light-transactional, message-oriented appli-

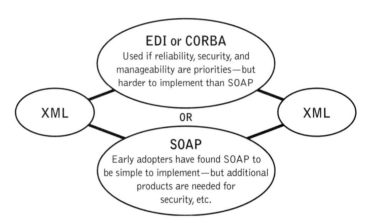

FIGURE 0-3    Using Other Architectures until Web Services Mature.

cation that does not have those strong requirements, the Web services SOAP protocol can be used.

Another approach that can help remedy some of today's shortcomings is to supplement Web services standards with "point" product (other hardware and software combinations that supplement Web services protocols). For instance, if a Web services administrator required additional security for a particular application, she could install add-on security software. IBM, Hewlett-Packard, RSA, Forum Systems, and others provide such security software. And if an enterprise wished to enhance the manageability of its Web services, third parties such as IBM, HP, webMethods, and others offer Web services management software. Routing shortcomings could also be handled by specialized hardware and software available from a number of suppliers. (Supplier offerings are discussed later in the vendor comparison chapter.)

## When Will My Organization Need to Be Ready to Deploy Web Services?

When will Web services standards and extensions be mature enough to be used in real-world production environments?" Research reported in this book shows that some

Web services applications are ready today to be deployed in
certain types of application environments (message-based
with low security and low transaction-rate requirements).
To expand the reach of Web services in the marketplace,
new standards will have to evolve around security, reliable
messaging, routing, transaction-handling, performance tuning, and more. Most of these issues are being dealt with
accordingly by standards committees. Meanwhile, vendors,
the open-source community, and consortia are stepping forward with their own programs to fill the gap.

The accompanying Gartner Group chart (Figure 0–4) illustrates this analyst firm's view of the emergence of Web services over the next several years.

Note how the Gartner prognostication emphasizes the
important role of UDDI registries in helping drive the
acceptance of Web services. This theme will be echoed often
in this book. In many cases UDDI is not used because a
large public UDDI directory does not yet exist. Until formal,
public UDDI registries come into being, Web services will
fall short of its true commercial potential.

On the personal computing side, personal Web services
applications are just starting to come to market. While businesses will need to wait at least two years to exploit UDDI

**2001** Web services tooling delivered. Developers buy new on-site
development tools, begin building vital Web services.

**2002** Business Web services begin to appear in large numbers. Mass-
connected B2C Web services already in place.

**2003** UDDI Registry adoption grows in significance. Private registries
proliferate to support private exchanges. Government use of Web
accelerates significantly.

**2004** Business adoption of Web services-based models. Services-centered
computing enters adolescence. Private registries still dominate
revenue-generation models, and channel opportunities are
commonplace. Forty percent of financial services transactions
leverage Web services model. Thirty five percent of government
services are delivered as Web services.

**2005** Public UDDI Registries gain attention as public exchanges.
Dynamic services gain more attention.

FIGURE 0-4   When Will Your Organization Need to Adopt Web
Services? *Source:* "Web Services: Software as Service Comes Alive,"
Daryl Plummer, October 2001. Used by Permission.

registries, personal Web services applications are ready to go and are coming to market today.

## Vendor Selection Criteria

The trade press and some Web sites portray the forthcoming move to a Web services model of application development and deployment as a "battle" between vendors—usually between Microsoft (with its C# development language and .NET application development environment) and Sun™ (with its Java™ platform/language basis). But Web services has more to do with creating applications *compatibility* between vendors than it does with whether Microsoft will dominate Sun (or any other vendor) on the basis of development-language choice. Remember this: if vendors do not focus on *interoperability* and *compatibility* between their respective Web services platforms, then the whole concept of Web services program-to-program communications will not work.

Instead of just a battle between Java platform supporters and Microsoft .NET platform supporters, the forthcoming Web services competition will be based on other factors, including:

- *The fullness of a particular vendor's support for Web services standards.* The vendors that offer the richest support for evolved Web services standards will win more business.
- *Ease of development and deployment.* The companies that create the easiest ways to build and deploy Web services-based applications will obtain the largest market share. To win in Web services, a supplier has to offer a richly integrated platform that has a good selection of developmental tools, optimized hardware, and value-added extensions (such as wireless device support or personalization). Conversely, the companies that offer the least amount of compatibility with Web services standards and the poorest toolsets for implementing

those standards will most likely garner the least market share.

- *Services.* Several professional services firms are already building Web services expertise in order to assist enterprises in building Web services-based applications. And many ASPs also recognize that a significant revenue opportunity exists for those who develop and host Web services type applications.

The "big winners" among vendors of platforms and tools will be those who make it easy to develop Web services applications, incorporate other value-added software (such as personalization, security, or business process management) and who either directly or through business partnerships offer professional design, develop, and deployment services.

The final third of this book is dedicated to describing the various Web service product offerings of the leading competitors in the Web services market. Readers will see that Web services involves a lot more than just adherence to certain Web services protocol and registry standards—it involves the creation of entire, integrated product suites that make it easier for application developers to build and deploy highly functional Web services-based solutions.

## Three Approaches

Anecdotal examples in this book describe the best approaches used by various enterprises to implement Web services today. This book also identifies three approaches that facilitate the building and deployment of Web services-based applications. To get started on building a Web services application environment your options are to:

1. Use an application-server approach. (An application server is a turnkey environment that has tools and utilities for building Web services applications—usually optimized for a particular underlying systems/operating system platform.) Application servers can be all-inclusive (hardware, software, and services) or they

can be software platforms that can run on a particular hardware platform or across multiple different platform types.

2. Find a la carte tools and utilities or open-source software and then glue various components together in order to create Web services. (This involves far more integration work by the IT department than the previous approach but can be significantly less costly than purchasing an entire application server environment).

3. Employ a professional services firm to assist with Web services application development and/or with training an existing staff on how to build Web services applications.

## Chapter Summary

Web services represent a new, standards-based way of creating application programs that can work cooperatively with other application programs, regardless of the platform or program languages used between the two. By enabling this loosely coupled approach to cross-platform, program-to-program communications, Web services are expected to change the way that various enterprises will compete in the future. (Among many other benefits, Web services will help lower development costs and improve market/competitive response times.) Hence it is extremely important that business executives and strategists gain a basic understanding of what Web services are and how they work. (*Failure to do so will leave the enterprises of some executives vulnerable to attack by more nimble competitors and may also result in inefficiencies in application development and in business process flow.*)

The benefits of building Web services are many. The biggest payback centers on development-cost reduction and rapid response to changing market or competitive situations. But other benefits also hold great potential for adopters of Web services, such as being able to use existing intellectual property to create new revenue opportunities (e.g., applications that have already been written for internal use can be made available on a charge basis). Nine distinct benefits that can be derived using Web services were described in this chapter.

Web services are still evolving and have some "maturity" issues (gotchas) to deal with. The good news is that the *foundation* for Web services application design and deployment *is in place* thanks to the standardization of XML for data/document presentation/manipulation; UDDI registries; and WSDL templates, SOAP APIs, and HTTP protocols. The current shortcomings in security, manageability, reliability, routing, and transaction handling can be dealt with using third-party software designed to supplement the existing Web services protocols.

Early adopters have other options for building a Web services-oriented architecture. Other approaches to distributed computing, such as CORBA and EDI, can be used to send and receive XML and other data in a secure and reliable manner. Many early adopters are using these other approaches for passing XML data in the short term, but they are planning to use Web services standard protocols such as SOAP and WSDL over time to replace architectures such as CORBA and EDI that are more complex and difficult to program.

When should your organization be prepared to adopt Web services? A strong argument can be made that Web services can be used successfully today in certain application processing environments (in which the key aspect is message passing or data sharing). But Web services are probably not, at this juncture, appropriate for highly transactional environments where secure and reliable communications are required, unless augmented with third-party hardware or software.

Also be aware that one of the key elements of Web services is a registry service called UDDI—and public UDDI directories/registries will not mature for a few years. Without them, cooperative applications will have trouble finding each other, thus preventing Web services from living up to their full potential. Research conducted by the Gartner Group combined with research conducted by this author suggests that mature UDDI directories are still several years off. This means that your organization has a few years to build prototypes using SOAP and WSDL (while allowing public UDDI registries to develop).

There are three approaches to deploying Web services: (1) partner with an application server vendor; (2) do it yourself using tools and utilities provided by various vendors or standards organizations; and (3) find a professional services partner who can implement Web services for you. This book takes a close look at product and services offerings from various vendors that fit into each of these categories.

As you evaluate Web services vendors, realize that competition will be based on three factors: (1) the depth of the Web services offering (as in: does it implement the Web services protocols and services correctly?); (2) the breadth of additional products that help developers design, build, deploy, and manage Web services offerings; and (sometimes) (3) the availability of professional services. These are the considerations that business executives should weigh when determining which vendor's products to utilize and when developing Web services-based business and technology strategies.

# part I

# A Business Executive Primer on Web Services

**1**

# What Are "Web Services"?

Key Insights:

- Web services are a distributed computing architecture that features the use of loosely coupled applications that perform services for one another. They feature a new way to perform program-to-program communications that allow applications to communicate with each other regardless of which application language was used to create an application—and regardless of what systems platform and operating environment is being used.
- Basic Web services consist of UDDI, WSDL, and SOAP.
- More complete Web services implementations include application development environments, business process management software, Web/portal development products, connectors/adapters for legacy applications, and more—all highly integrated with Web services protocols and registry services.

**21**

Web services are a distributed computing architecture—as are Common Object Request Broker (CORBA), Advanced Program-to-Program Communications (APPC), Electronic Data Interchange (EDI), and dozens of other preceding architectures.

The purpose of a distributed computing architecture is to enable programs in one environment to communicate and share data/content with programs in another environment. In the past, programmers have had to tell one application program where to go to find another cooperative program (known as "tightly coupling" applications). These programmers have had to maintain these programmatic links over the useful life of the applications that they have written. Creating these "hard-wired" links is complicated, cumbersome, and human resource intensive.

Now, imagine that a new distributed computing architecture has come along. And imagine that instead of requiring people (programmers) to establish and maintain program-to-program links, the applications themselves could automatically find cooperative programs to work with. And imagine that this new architecture allowed programmers to rapidly assemble complex applications merely by tying together application modules. And imagine that this new architecture allowed businesses to create or respond to competitive pressure more rapidly than ever before. And imagine that this new architecture allowed software to be delivered as a pay-as-you-go service. And so on.

Web services makes use of a program-to-program communications process called "loosely coupled." And by using this approach the amount of human involvement in building applications can be minimized. And the Web services protocols themselves are simpler and more straightforward to use than those of preceding architectures. Web services holds the promise of making programming vastly simpler.

But also consider this: loosely coupling applications has another important effect. Businesses can link strings of applications together to deliver new services to market—on the fly. And businesses can use Web services to market their existing nonstrategic software if they so desire. (In this book

I identify nine different ways that Web services architecture allows businesses to restructure or modify their existing business models.) In short, Web services will change the way we build and use information systems—and will thus change the underlying business models upon which many enterprises currently operate.

Web services are one of the most significant advances in computing architecture over the past 30 years. Accordingly, it would be wise to become familiar with Web services architecture and concepts because it is highly likely that Web services will have a significant impact on the way your enterprise conducts business in the future.

Web services:

- Are designed to enable application modules (objects) to communicate with other application modules. Once connected, service applications provide transactional or computational services.
- Make use of a common data/information formatting scheme known as eXtensible Markup Language (XML) to share data.
- Applications make use of certain Web standards (UDDI, WSDL, and SOAP) for registry and program-to-program communications purposes.
- Use the Internet as the common network backbone.

Unstated but assumed in these brief definitions is that Web services are designed to be platform and language independent. This means that applications that use Web services are able to communicate with one another regardless of the underlying operating environment, system platform, or programming language being used.

Also unstated but assumed is that readers understand the concept of "object-oriented programming." Applications can be written as discrete, self-contained "object modules"—application "blocks" that can service the needs of one application and, if appropriate, can also be reused to provide functions for other applications.

> For instance, if a programmer were to write a calculator program, it could be written as a module and made available to a spreadsheet program, a customized transaction program, a mortgage amortization program, or any other program that could logically make use of a calculator. The point is that a calculator program has to be written only once (not constantly recreated) and can then be "bolted-onto," coupled, or reused with other applications in order to perform calculation services.

The use of "objects" is a fundamental concept in Web services, because it enables the assembly of large, compound applications faster than by today's monolithic methods. And, because programmers do not need to constantly recreate objects from scratch (they just plug in the appropriate object and away they go), application development will be less expensive.

**Another Way of Defining What Web Services Do: Consider Publish, Find, and Bind**

Here is another way to understand how Web services work. Web services directories and protocols essentially serve three functions: publish, find, and bind. To use Web services, applications are:

- *Published* in a common UDDI directory (such that cooperating applications can find each other);
- *Found* (using WSDL protocols that can locate Web services applications and determine if those applications can work with the source application); and
- *Bound* (a communications link between the two applications is established, so that a service—such as performing some sort of calculation or transaction—can be rendered using SOAP protocols).

These three service elements and their relationship to requester, broker, and provider services are illustrated in Figure 1–1.

In this illustration a service requester is either you or your source application. The requester initiates the request for a Web service application. The Service Provider is the Web services application itself. The Service Broker can be a company that provides lists and information about Web ser-

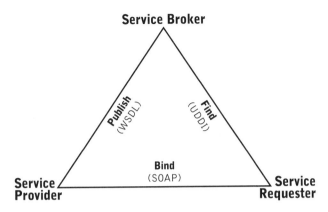

FIGURE 1-1    Web Services: Publish, Find, Bind.

vices programs, or a Service Broker can refer to the programmatic process that helps locate an application and helps the two cooperating applications determine how to best communicate.

**The Author's Personal Definition of Web Services**

In this author's view, after taking into consideration all of these data points, Web services are a new class of *cross-platform program-to-program communications* that enable loosely coupled applications to easily find each other, to easily and dynamically establish parameters that enable similar or disparate programs to work together cooperatively, and enable them to communicate in an automated, unattended fashion over the Internet.

"Web services are applications that make use of registry and communications standards to work together in a dynamic (fluid) manner (where one application provides transactional, messaging, or computational 'services' for another). These applications make use of an agreed-to format (XML or some variant of XML) for presenting information and data; and they use Web services standards for finding service applications (UDDI), negotiating how to send and receive information (WSDL), binding communications sessions (SOAP), and then transferring that information over the Internet (HTTP)."

# A Basic Web Services Architecture

Earlier sections in this chapter have dealt with defining Web services and describing how they work (from a program-to-program perspective). A closer look reveals that Web services pass content between applications using a common format known as XML; Web services use a registry (UDDI), a template (WSDL), and a programmatic interface (SOAP) to enable applications to find and interact with each other; and they use a common network (the Internet) to transport information and data between cooperating applications (see Figure 1–2).

These are considered to be the basic building blocks of Web services architecture. But, as stated previously, the benefits of Web services architecture can be maximized if used in conjunction with business process management software to help streamline business workflow. And, by making application program development easier and linking application development with Web services protocols, more Web services applications can be developed. The next section

| Format | **XML**<br>(Format) | A common format for presenting data and information. This data can be easily manipulated to meet the presentation needs of the requester application. | |
|---|---|---|---|
| Services | **UDDI**<br>(Publish)<br><br>A directory service that lists applications that can provide services. | **WSDL**<br>(Find)<br><br>A protocol that enables applications to find a service and to agree on how data and services are to be shared and rendered. | **SOAP**<br>(Bind)<br><br>A protocol that enables applications to agree on how data and services are to be communicated. |
| Network | **The Internet**<br><br>The Internet, using TCP/IP and other communications/networking protocols, serves as the common network for Web-enabled applications. | | |

FIGURE 1-2    Critical Elements of a Basic Web Services Architecture.

describes how application development environments, Web (portal) development environments, mobile computing, and business process management software can all be used to create a highly integrated Web services development environment.

## A Complete Web Services Architecture

A recent Gartner Group "Perspective" on Web services implementations states:

> "The Web services vision will be less than optimal if it is not introduced as a complete vision for dealing with aspects such as services registry, messaging, trading-partner specifications and industry standards."
> *Source:* http://mass25.mbinteractive.com/mass/bedemir.dll/ b12100720=1. "Web Services: Software as Service Comes Alive," Daryl Plummer, October 2001. Used by Permission.

In other words, far more is involved in building a Web services architecture than the "basic" architecture described in the previous section. A number of companies—including BEA, Hewlett-Packard, IBM, Microsoft, Sun, and others— have combined various development tools, application accelerators, specialized applications, and integration services to offer a more complete Web services architecture than described above. These environments contain additional architectural elements that are useful in building very robust, user-friendly Web services environments for small, medium, and large enterprises.

The example presented here is based on IBM's WebSphere product set (Figure 1–3). It is a particularly robust Internet application server environment, though not the only such solution available on the market today. Microsoft, BEA, HP, Oracle, Sun, and others have competitive products (though potentially not as broad as IBM's offering from a cross-platform integration perspective). All of these vendors and more will be covered in greater depth later in this book.

SIDEBAR 1-1
## AN EXAMPLE: IBM'S WEBSPHERE PLATFORM

Although Microsoft, BEA, and others offer somewhat similar products and services, IBM's WebSphere platform is a good starting point for evaluating the broad range of products and tools that can be used to build a robust Web services environment, because it contains all of the basic products and tools for creating a "basic Web services environment" (as described in the preceding section) plus many extensions needed to better integrate systems and applications with Web services applications on disparate platforms; or to present data to a wide range of different device types; or to deploy applications across multiple systems environments; or to secure and manage Web services application environments.

IBM's Web services protocols and directory services are hosted in various products and development tools within the company's WebSphere product set. The company separates its WebSphere offerings into three classes:

- Application accelerators (programs and tools that help customers develop applications more quickly);

- Development, Presentation, Deployment, and Integration extensions (IBM calls these offerings WebSphere "Foundation extensions"); and,

- Web Application Serving and Integration services (IBM calls these offerings the WebSphere "Foundation").

These three classes contain software that helps developers to build Web services applications and also to build personalized user experiences and customized portals. They also include software that helps manage and secure entire WebSphere environments. Figure 1–3 lists a number of IBM's WebSphere-related software offerings.

The preceding section described how a basic Web services architecture can be built by settling on a common presentation format, using common program-to-program protocols over a common network (the Internet). Figure 1–3 illustrates how IBM extends its Web services architecture by including a wealth of systems software, development tools, Web tools (for personalization and presentation), integration tools, and utilities, as well as application development environments and applications (such as Lotus Domino) that can be tuned or modified to work in a Web services mode.

---

### Accelerators

Lotus Domino (helps build collaborative and messaging applications);
WebSphere Commerce Suite; WebSphere Business-to-Business Integrator;
MQ Series Workflow

### Foundation Extensions

Capabilities for security and systems management as well as for development,
presentation, and deployment. Products include:

Build:
VisualAge for Java (for Java application development); WebSphere Studio;
WebSphere HomePage; WebSphere Business Components

Presentation:
VisualAge Generator; Application Rules (for deploying applications based
on business rules); WebSphere Personalization (rules-based filtering to
tailor Web experiences for visitors); WebSphere Portal Server (create
Web portals); WebSphere Voice Server (based on VoiceXML to present
data via voice over Web)

Deploy:
WebSphere Transcoding Publisher; WebSphere Edge Server; WebSphere
Site Analyzer; MQ Series Integrator; Tivoli Policy Director

### Foundation

Consists of WebSphere Application Servers (server platforms) and MQ
Series messaging products.

---

FIGURE 1-3   IBM's WebSphere Architecture. *Source:* Derived from
http://www-4.ibm.com/cgibin/software/track3.cgi?file=/software/info/
websphere/products/index.html&S_TACT=100AWW10&S_CMP
=campaign. Used by Permission.

Other elements also help to create a "complete" Web services environment, including:

1. *Systems management* and *security.*

2. The user experience (including *personalization, portal
   graphics*).

3. *Support for multiple device types* (PDAs, smart phones,
   other mobile devices, desktops, workstations) using
   various interfaces (such as data-to-voice) for information presentation/relay.

4. *Business process management/workflow* (Web services can
   be implemented without paying attention to workflow
   and business process management software, but, to
   support hundreds or thousands of Web services sessions, Web services implementers should consider

using business process management programs and tools in order to maximize the effectiveness and efficiency of Web-based applications).

5. *Integration* (not only between disparate systems but also between application environments).

The IBM WebSphere example used in this section (similar in architectural structure to products of Microsoft and other companies) illustrates that implementing a complete Web services environment involves a lot more than just servicing requests for application services from requestor applications!

## Chapter Summary

There are many definitions of Web services, but almost all of them contain the following elements:

- Web services is a distributed computing architecture that features the use of loosley coupled applications.
- Web services are designed to enable application modules (objects) to communicate with other application modules. Once connected, service applications provide messaging, transactional, or computational services.
- Web services make use of a common data-presentation/information-formatting scheme known as eXtensible Markup Language (XML) to share data.
- Web services applications make use of certain Web standards (UDDI, WSDL, and SOAP) for registry and program-to-program communications purposes.
- Web services use the Internet as the common network backbone.

This author personally defines Web services as a traditional form of cross-vendor program-to-program communications that uses the Internet as a common network to enable applications to communicate with each other. Only Web services uses a loosely coupled approach, as opposed to hard-coding applications together.

Web services can be quite simple and straightforward (programs that request content or information to be shared over a common network); or quite complex—including business process management, personalization, systems integration, and other aspects related to creating large, secure, manageable networked environments. Business managers need to understand that Web services are:

1. A common agreed-to format that applications can use to exchange information and data;

2. A means for applications to be published, found, and bound such that applications can find each other and work cooperatively together;

3. A way to network multiple, sometimes disparate systems together to share data, information, and services (the Internet provides this).

But these are just the basic elements for building Web services. Large enterprise environments, wishing to make use of many services and support hundreds or thousands of users, must also consider other elements such as business process management; cross-platform integration; Web and application development tools; and other programs, tools, and utilities. A broader view of Web services architecture includes much more.

Building a complex Web services environment that includes business process management, personalization, security, and other integrated products can prove to be a daunting task, especially for many small and mid-sized businesses. Fortunately, several companies including IBM, Microsoft, Sun, and others build complete "application server" environments that integrate other important software with Web services software.

# 2

# What Are Program-to-Program Communications?

Chapter 1 described Web services as a type of program-to-program communications. It showed how newly evolving standards are being created to enable applications to be published, found, and bound in a manner that makes it possible to share information across diverse and disparate systems/application platforms. It also presented a much larger picture of Web services as part of an overall architecture that can lead to easier application development, work/business flow efficiencies, improved application support for mobile users, and much, much more.

This chapter takes a closer look at program-to-program communications. It describes how this type of communications works. It then describes various program-to-program communications architectures and some of their respective strengths and weaknesses. It concludes with reasons that Web services will overcome the pitfalls experienced by previous architectures and become the method of choice for program-to-program communications.

## What Are Program-to-Program Communications?

The general idea behind program-to-program communications is to allow one application to work cooperatively with another, usually over a communications network. To do this, applications must be able to:

- *Share data.* This necessitates that a common content/ format be used between each application. Past examples of this common content/format include IBM's Document Content Architecture (DCA) and attempts at creating industry standard forms using Electronic Document Interchange (EDI) formats with ASCII content.

- *Initiate "calls" to each other.* Calls are usually based on verbs, such as "send," "receive," "open," "close," and other action-word activities that enable applications to share files and information. These calls are implemented using a common programmatic interface known as an *Application Program Interface (API),* consisting essentially of verbs that applications use to communicate with each other.

- *Communicate with each other over a network.* Programs need to be able to send and receive data and information over a common network (which involves using a common communications protocol such as TCP/IP, SNA, or other networking protocols).

Traditional distributed applications have communicated in the past by using a common format, a common API, and a common network, as illustrated in Figure 2–1. This figure shows that:

- both systems support the same format/content (in this case it's XML or HTML);
- both systems support the same application program interface; and
- both systems support a common network (in this case the Internet) in order to communicate.

In Figure 2–1, application "A" sends a request for data or information to application "B." Because the computer platform that "B" runs on uses the same underlying network (the Internet), the same programmatic interfaces (APIs), and uses the same way of reading and presenting content (based

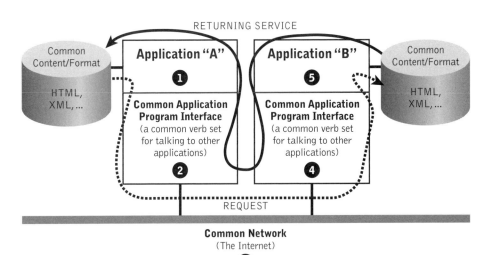

FIGURE 2-1    Program-to-Program Communications Basics.

on XML or HTML), the two applications are able to easily communicate and share data. Web services use this same basic approach (common format, common APIs, common network) to enable one application to provide messaging, transactional, or computational services for another.

Web services behave very much like traditional program-to-program communications. A "requester" application sends out a request for a service (in the Web services world this request is sent to a UDDI registry that contains information on where that service can be found). Once the service is located, WSDL negotiates between applications and establishes the rules for transferring/sharing information. SOAP binds the communications session, and the HTTP protocol is used to send information back and forth over the Internet. Chapter 3 covers Web services architecture in greater technological detail (for readers who wish to understand how Web services APIs, content, and registries actually work).

## Previous Program-to-Program Communications Architectures Have Met with Limited Success

If you've been involved in the computer industry for a while, you'll probably be asking yourself why this talk of Web services sounds vaguely familiar. Consider this: for over two decades Information System (IS) managers have sought a means to enable applications to work transparently and cooperatively with other applications, irrespective of vendor platform, programming language, and operating system. These executives have heard and seen multiple schemes by many vendors that were designed to provide cross-platform program-to-program communications.

Against this background, Web services looks and sounds awfully familiar. It promises to be a cross-platform program-to-program architecture that will enable various programs on disparate information systems using completely different programming languages to work together seamlessly. It offers to use the ubiquitous Internet for network connection; and it is based on Internet standards for programmatic interfaces and directory look-ups.

So the big question for IS managers and business systems executives is, "Why will this set of Internet Web services standards actually succeed when other similar approaches in the past have failed (or at least not garnered tremendous market acceptance)?"

**Examples:
Previous
Approaches**

Information Systems executives have been discussing program-to-program communications since the early 1980s, when IBM introduced its Systems Application Architecture (SAA). This distributed computing architecture had elements similar to the current Web services directories and protocols:

- IBM's Document Content Architecture (DCA) was used to create a common content/format (just as XML does).
- Logical Unit 6.2 (LU6.2—an application program interface also known as APPC for Advanced Program-to-Program communications) was designed to let applications talk to each other (just as WSDL does); IBM's peer-to-peer Physical Unit 2.1 (PU 2.1—a peer systems communications protocol) was used to bind sessions (similar to what SOAP does).
- All of this was done over a network called Systems Network Architecture (SNA) using SNA protocols for data transport—as opposed to a network called the Internet using the HTTP protocol for data transport.

Over the years, tens of thousands of transaction-oriented applications have been written using these protocols and programmatic interfaces. But for small- and mid-sized businesses, writing LU 6.2-based programs and driving them over an SNA network proved too complex. Consequently, these protocols and APIs were related to uses in large enterprises and between high-end transaction-oriented midrange minicomputers and mainframe computers.

Over the years, new variations on the same theme have come to market in the form of "object-oriented programming" or "distributed computing," or the "Common Object

Request Broker Architecture" (CORBA), IIOP (Internet Inter ORB Protocol), DCOM (Distributed Component Object Model), and any of a number of other architectural approaches. Many of these approaches have met with some success, but mostly in intranet/extranet situations (not over the public, far-reaching Internet).

Over time, most of these approaches have run into issues that have kept them from being more broadly adopted for cross-platform program-to-program communications. Some of these issues are related to architectural design and complexity, to binary compatibility, to requirements for homogeneous operating-environment, and to concerns about vendor proprietary lock-in (buyers worried that committing to some of these architectures would limit their choices of equipment and operating systems).

One of the best explanations of past failures can be found in this somewhat technical description of market behavior by IBM's Web Services Architecture Team:

> Previous attempts at distributed computing (CORBA, Distributed Smalltalk, Java RMI) have yielded systems where the coupling between various components in a system is too tight to be effective for low-overhead, ubiquitous B2B e-business over the Internet. These approaches require too much agreement and shared context among business systems from different organizations to be reliable for open, low-overhead B2B e-business.
>
> Meanwhile, the current trend in the application space is moving away from tightly coupled monolithic systems and towards systems of loosely coupled, dynamically bound components. Systems built with these principles are more likely to dominate the next generation of e-business systems, with flexibility being the overriding characteristic of their success.

Further, the IBM Web Services Architecture Team indicate that they believe that the concept of Web services will succeed:

> We [IBM] believe that applications will be based on
> compositions of services discovered and marshaled dynamically
> at runtime (just-in-time integration of services). Service
> (application) integration becomes the innovation of the next
> generation of e-business, as businesses move more of their
> existing IT applications to the Web, taking advantage of e-
> portals and e-marketplaces and leveraging new technologies,
> such as XML.
> *Source:* http://www-106.ibm.com/developerworks/library/w-ovr/.
> Used by Permission.

In other words, previous attempts to build cross-platform
program-to-program applications were too cumbersome to
build and deploy. The team further states that the new trend
is toward more fluid "dynamically bound components"—
that is, toward applications that can establish contact, share
information, and then break contact after they have provided a transactional or computational service.

Web services will succeed, then, because they are based on
agreed-to program-to-program communications standards
that are easier to implement than previous architectures
(because they consist of loosely coupled transactions rather
than code-intensive hard-wired transactions). This ease of
use combined with an ability to provide services "as
needed" in a just-in-time fashion for other applications will
ultimately lead to the success of this newly evolving Web
services approach to programming.

## Why Program-to-Program Communications Using Web Services Will Become the Industry Standard

Another way to compare past and present approaches is to
consider the following:

- In the past, sharing data and information was difficult
  because various vendors used proprietary or dissimilar
  formats that prevented easy, effortless sharing of infor-

mation. The industry now has a common "format" for presenting data called HTML (Hypertext Markup Language) and a new variant of this "markup language" used for presenting and manipulating data (XML).

- The industry now has a common way to network applications (the Internet). In the past, a plethora of communications protocols (SNA, Bisynch, Asynch, OSI, IPX/SPX, and others) essentially precluded applications from disparate communications environments from working together. Today, the Internet provides a common means for applications to reach each other using TCP/IP protocols. Vendors now have a common network path (the Internet) that is supported by almost every leading software vendor for sharing information over a network.

- Almost every leading vendor of hardware, software, and applications has now embraced (or strategically committed to) the use of three newly evolved Internet standards (UDDI, WSDL, and SOAP) that enable data and information to be manipulated and shared over the Internet. Application builders finally have vendor commitments to implement the protocols and directory services developers need to in order to build Web services applications that can work across disparate platforms.

- The industry has formed its own interoperability testing organization to ensure that Web services work.

SIDEBAR 2-1

## THE WEB SERVICES INTEROPERABILITY ORGANIZATION

In February 2002, Microsoft Corp. and International Business Machines Corp. along with cofounders Fujitsu, SAP AG, and Accenture Ltd. announced that they had formed a consortium to make sure that the Web services products that each company develops will interoperate. This consortium, the Web Services Interoperabilty Organization, shows that IBM, Microsoft, cofounders, and fellow members such as Intel, BEA, Compaq Computer Corporation, Oracle, Toshiba, and Hewlett-Packard understand the importance of cross-platform interoperabilty and are willing to work together to achieve program-to-program communications across diverse systems platforms.

Also of interest, vendor organizations have been joined in this effort by early-adopter and leading-edge customers such as DaimlerChrysler AG, Ford Motor Company, Reed Elsevier Plc, and Reuters Group Plc. These user organizations are expected to help the consortium examine and emphasize business-related issues along with technology-related issues that pertain to how Web services are designed and deployed.

Without such a consortium there is a risk that vendors could interpret Web services standards differently, leading to incompatibilities between vendor implementations that would preclude interoperability. The consortium aims to provide a forum where vendors can work out issues that may lead to such incompatibilities.

Another role of the consortium is to provide education and guidance for adopters of Web services architecture.

At the time of this writing, Sun Microsystems had not agreed to join the consortium. But it is reasonable to expect that Sun will join the consortium at some point to ensure that its Web services implementation is consistent with those of other vendors. And it is reasonable to expect, too, that customers will demand that Sun join the consortium to ensure that their voices are heard as standards are refined and interoperability issues are addressed.

Because the industry has been able to overcome issues related to how to package and communicate data, and because every leading vendor has announced support for Web services standards, Web services stand a chance of succeeding where other previous architectures have not.

## Chapter Summary

This chapter described program-to-program communications in greater detail. Essentially, program-to-program communications is a way for applications to work cooperatively with other applications, using:

1. Some method of locating a cooperative application;

2. Application program interfaces (verb sets) for communicating with other applications and databases; and,

3. Common network protocols (an agreed-to method of transporting data between systems).

Today's Web services follow this model. XML is the means to create and present content in a consistent and readable form. WSDL is a template that helps describe *how* applications can communicate with each other. SOAP is an API (application program interface) that allows programs to talk with each other. And the Internet has become the common network environment (with HTTP as the common transport protocol).

UDDI allows public and private programs to find each other. [In the past, programmers "told" most applications where to go to get the service they needed (by hard coding the ports or addresses where service programs could be found). UDDI enables requester applications to search the Internet (or an intra- or extranet) to find the best service application to meet the requester's need]. In this respect, UDDI is a new and different function now found in distributed computing architecture.

After describing program-to-program communications, this chapter considered other program-to-program schema of the past. It concluded that Web services will succeed where other approaches have not. What is different this time is that:

- Building the connections between cooperating applications is far more straightforward and far easier than ever before. Previous attempts had to deal with different network types and APIs and conflicting vendor interests as they attempted to standardize this form of program-to-program communications. With the use of the Internet as a common network—and with standards developed to work specifically over the Internet across development-language environments—Web services has a strong advantage over previous architectural attempts at cross-platform program-to-program communications.

- All of the industry's major hardware and software vendors have endorsed this newly evolved, standards-based Web services approach. Several vendors have made Web services central to their product and services strategies over the next several years and have committed the resources to build and market Web services-based solutions.

The primary obstacles to Web services are related to delays in standards committees as well as the prospect for partial implementations or incompatibilities on the vendor's side. Market demand from early adopters indicates that significant pressure will be put on both camps. Demand from buyers and users will pressure standards bodies to get standards out of committee and into the market (or users will create their own solutions). Vendors who are slow to respond with products that enable their customers to stay competitive may find themselves losing customers to vendors who do offer rich Web services products.

But is this approach a "sure thing"? Should your company consider changing its approach to programming and invest heavily in Web services application development? Conventional wisdom has it that there's no such thing as a sure thing—but with such as strong commitment being exhibited by all of the major vendors of computer hardware and software to this architecture, Web services architecture looks pretty darn close.

# 3

# How Do Specific Web Services Technologies Work?

**In This Chapter:**

- A closer look at the specific technologies (XML, UDDI, WSDL, SOAP) that comprise Web services
- A big surprise—Web services can be architected without using formal Web services standards

**Key Insights:**

- XML is extremely important in the Web services scheme of things because XML provides the wrapper in which readable and manipulatable data can be passed between disparate applications.
- Web services mechanisms such as UDDI, WSDL, and SOAP are immature from a reliability, security, manageability, routing, and transaction handling perspective when compared to other communications architectures such as CORBA, EDI, and COM. Hence, many early adopters are using other communications architectures to pass XML data until formal Web services standards mature a bit more.

C hapter 2 described the concept of program-to-program communications in greater detail. It showed how Web services program-to-program communications actually works by illustrating how: (1) data is packaged in a common format that can be read by cooperating applications (XML); (2) programs are able to find each other (UDDI); (3) programs are able to share information and negotiate with each other (WSDL); (4) programs are able to commence communications and transfer data (SOAP); and (5) programs use a common network (the Internet) for program-to-program communications.

This chapter takes a closer look at all of these Web services technologies. How do they work? What specifically do they do? What additional standards efforts are underway to support the basic Web services protocols? This chapter concludes with a discussion about other options available to your organization that can be used to compliment or replace Web services protocols, registries, and formats. Many of the research examples (account scenarios/anecdotes) contained later in this book show that early adopters are not using all of the Web services protocols and services in the initial solutions that they have built. This chapter examines alternate approaches that are being used until Web services protocols become more mature.

## Specific Web Services Technologies

Probably the most important technology being used to create Web services applications is XML. Previous sections have greatly simplified the role of XML as being a means to package and describe data, content, and format. For most business managers this definition is more than sufficient.

But some business managers may wish to understand how Web services technologies really work from a technical perspective. This section provides a little more depth in that respect. The following few sections "drill-down" in greater detail on Web services technologies and examine how XML, UDDI, WSDL, and SOAP really work. These sections also examine some of the other standards that are important for building Web services.

**XML: A Lot More Than Just Content/ Format**

For those familiar with XML specifications, there is a whole lot more involved in using XML standards to share data than I've indicated so far in this book. There are XML schema (presentation forms) that represent how various vertical industries would like to present data (such as invoices or other business document) to each other, there are specialized vocabularies that may need to be used, and there is core processing that needs to take place to interpret XML data.

How does XML work? XML is a recommendation about how to structure data—additional work goes into actually formatting that data for use across particular industries or between specific business partners. XML can tell a developer how to pass data—but schema need to be developed to present and share that data in a useful form between cooperating programs. (And at last count, there were about 900 schema that had been developed).

Here are a few examples of organizations that are helping to devise XML schema for their members in vertical industries:

- **RosettaNet**. RosettaNet is a consortium of supply-chain trading partners whose goal is to define the schema necessary to accomplish business trading partner collaborative activities. For instance, a maker of shoes may wish to use XML to share data about shoes with business partners. An XML schema could be developed that would enable that shoe maker to present data in such a way that it can automatically be dropped into a business partner's electronic product catalog with no human intervention necessary. Using a common schema saves time, helps suppliers match inventory to their distribution channels, and eliminates error-prone human intervention.

- **Open Buying on the Internet** (OBI). OBI is a consortium of companies dedicated to developing and deploying standards for Internet-based procurement. Part of OBIs charter is to develop an open vendor, platform neutral purchasing architecture that fosters interoperability among suppliers. To help do this, OBI has a special XML track in place to help define procurement procedures using XML language.

- **Organization for the Advancement of Structured Information Standards** (OASIS). OASIS is an international consortium focused on fostering the adoption of product-independent formats. XML is one such product-independent format. OASIS runs one of the industry's most valuable portals of information on XML (XML.Org) where visitors can obtain information on XML specifications such as vocabularies, schemas, and namespaces. Further, OASIS is helping to drive the Electronic Business XML (ebXML) initiative (a particular set of XML schema designed to create common forms for conducting electronic business).

All of these organizations (and several other independents as well as standards organizations) are helping to create XML-based forms that facilitate information transfer for their respective members.

**XML: Even More Technical Detail**

For those who still desire more information about how XML works with UDDI, WSDL, and SOAP, consider the following block diagram (courtesy of Bill Smith, director of Sun Microsystems' XML Technology Center).

SIDEBAR 3-1
## BILL SMITH'S COMMENTARY ON FIGURE 3–1

"The XML stack," as Smith put it, is comprised of six layers. The base layer, the Web framework, is comprised of basic Internet protocols such as TCP/IP, HTTP, and DNS. On top of that is the next horizontal layer, called XML core processing, which would be XML itself, including XSLT and schemas. The third layer is basic XML functions. The fourth layer, horizontal XML vocabularies, includes things like ebXML and Scalable Vector Graphics. This layer meets a horizontal dotted line. Above the dotted line live the horizontal Web services functions such as SOAP, UDDI, WSDL. The top layer is comprised of many smaller vertical language modules. Vertical industries such as OTA, RosettaNet, and eDub will define this layer (i.e., how to use the technology for business transactions).

| Vertical Language | Vertical Language | Vertical Language | Vertical Language | Vertical Language |
|---|---|---|---|---|
| Horizontal Web Services Functions | | | | |
| Horizontal XML Vocabularies | | | | |
| Basic XML Functions | | | | |
| Core XML Processing | | | | |
| Web Framework | | | | |

FIGURE 3-1    XML Is Far More Complex Than Just Content/Format. *Source:* http://java.sun.com/features/2001/10/xmlone.html. Used by Permission.

# The Roles of UDDI, WSDL, and SOAP

Smith's diagram (Figure 3–1) refers to "horizontal Web services." These services—such as UDDI, WSDL, and SOAP—help XML-based data to be communicated to other requester programs over the Internet.

Presented next is one of the briefest yet clearest definitions I've found of how XML, Web services protocols, and Web services registry services work together:

XML is the obvious choice for a standard way to represent data. Most Web Service-related specifications use XML for data representation, as well as XML Schemas to describe data types. The Simple Object Access Protocol (SOAP) defines a lightweight protocol for information exchange. Part of the SOAP specification defines a set of rules for how to use XML to represent data. Other parts of the SOAP specification define an extensible message format, conventions for representing remote procedure calls (RPCs) using the SOAP message format, and bindings to the HTTP protocol. (SOAP messages can be exchanged over other protocols, but the current specification only defines bindings for HTTP.) Microsoft anticipates that SOAP will be the standard message format for communicating with Web Services.

Given a Web Service, it would be nice to have a standard way to document what messages the Web Service accepts and generates—that is, to document the Web Service contract. A standard mechanism makes it easier for developers and developer tools to create and interpret contracts. The Web Services Description Language (WSDL) is an XML-based contract language jointly developed by Microsoft and IBM. We anticipate that WSDL will be widely supported by developer tools for creating Web Services.

*Note:* Over the past year Microsoft and IBM have proposed several contract languages: Service Description Language (SDL), SOAP Contract Language (SCL), and Network Accessible Services Specification Language (NASSL). While these are all superseded by WSDL, some early development tools use these languages. You might need to translate the provided contract into the contract language your development tool understands in order to consume a Web Service.

Developers will also need some way to discover Web Services. The Discovery Protocol (Disco) specification defines a discovery document format (based on XML) and a protocol for retrieving the discovery document, enabling developers to discover services at a known URL. However, in many cases the developer will not know the URLs where services can be found. Universal Description, Discovery, and Integration (UDDI) specifies a mechanism for Web Service providers to advertise the existence of their Web Services and for Web Service consumers to locate Web Services of interest.

*Source:* http://msdn.microsoft.com/library/default.asp?url=/library/en-us/dnwebsrv/html/websvcs_platform.asp. Used by Permission.

## Building a Web Services Architecture Using Some or None of the Formal Standards

In theory, the way that Web services are really supposed to work is that:

1. A source application makes a request to a directory service (UDDI) for a particular kind of application service. This directory steers the source application to one or many secondary Web services applications.

2. *The source application and the Web service application then need to agree on how they will communicate and exchange data.* Now that the source and secondary applications know about each other, they need to have a "discussion" about how to communicate. WSDL protocols help establish the parameters for the two applications to successfully exchange data and information.

3. Once agreement has been reached, the two applications cement the relationship (by binding communications together) and begin communicating (using SOAP protocols).

4. Data/information is transmitted over the Internet (using a "transport" protocol called HTTP).

I use the words "supposed to work" because of many of today's Web services applications use only a few of the protocols and registry services listed above.

- At this juncture, few public or private directories contain Web-enabled applications. The work-around for this situation is to write code that tells an application where to go to find a particular service (called "hard-coding"). In lieu of access to a very large and inclusive public UDDI directory, most Web services source applications are written in a manner that tells the source (requester) application where to find a particular service. Application programmers frequently "hard-code" application locations between two cooperative applications such that requester applications know where to go to obtain Web services.

- Many Web service applications written today make minimal use of WSDL and/or SOAP protocols. Instead, they use other APIs or other program-to-program models [such as Microsoft's Distributed Common Object Model (DCOM), or the OMG's CORBA interfaces]. The reason is usually that the enterprises writing the Web services applications already have code written in COM or DCOM or some other program model, and they find it expedient in the short term to use existing code in lieu of Web services protocols.

In other words, many of today's Web services applications are being written using hard-coding techniques to tell requester applications exactly where to find the services they need, and using application program interfaces other than Web services' SOAP and WSDL. At this juncture in time, using alternative approaches makes sense, because some of the alternative approaches are more robust than today's Web services protocols.

In many cases reusing applications that make use of non-Web services APIs is more expedient than rewriting existing code to be Web services compliant. Hence you will see in later chapters several examples of enterprises that have implemented Web services without using UDDI or WSDL or SOAP (but every one of them uses XML and HTTP).

In the longer term, in order to truly enable programs written in different programming languages to interoperate with other programs on disparate platforms, the common set of Web services APIs will have to be used. Until other aspects of Web services are enhanced (such as security and reliability), however, expect in many cases to see various first- and second-generation programmatic interfaces and architectures (such as COM or CORBA) being used to facilitate XML program-to-program communications.

## An Example: Using an Alternative Approach to UDDI for Finding Cooperative Applications

Another approach in lieu of using a UDDI directory service is to give the user the responsibility to find and link to the service he or she desires. Some "Web services" work by asking whether the user would like to be directed to a site where a transactional or computational service can be obtained. My favorite example of this approach is in Microsoft's Windows XP operating environment.

Have you ever received an e-mail from a friend with a file attachment that was in some file format that you didn't recognize? If you are like many people, you may have e-mailed your friend back and asked what format his or her document was stored as.

You would then have to go to the Web and find the appropriate "reader" in order to be able to view the document that was sent by your friend.

When this scenario unfolds under Microsoft's Windows XP operating environment, a Web service application is automatically activated when you try and read a file type that your system doesn't know. This application essentially says "Would you like to go to the Web to find a reader that can help you read the file that your friend just sent you?" If you answer yes, the program makes a call to a Web site with hundreds of file extensions (a file extension is represented by a dot and three letters that follow the document/file name that you have received—in a Microsoft Word document, for instance, this extension would be ".doc"). You then chose the appropriate file extension; the site helps you find the reader that you need; and voilá—you can now finally read the document or file that your friend has sent to you.

This example shows how applications can be written to provide services for you (albeit in this case the whole transaction was highly manual). And it shows how important having common formats is (because the failure to have a reader capable of reading your friend's document or file caused you to have to go through extra effort in order to read that file). The bottom line in this example is that the Web service requester application knew where to go to help you find the reader that you needed to view your friend's file/document—thus providing a valuable service for you (in this case, this service was provided in a semiautomated fashion). Longer term, this type of transaction could be wholly automated using UDDI, WSDL, and SOAP.

The preceding example provides a very simple and straightforward example of how a nonautomated Web service can work. A simple "requester program" went to a *known Web address* to obtain a service. This address was "known" by the requester program because a programmer put its address in the requester program (the programmer "hard-coded" a location to turn to in order to obtain a service). Once connected to the Web service site, the requester program asked a service program to help find a "reader" for file extensions that the user could not read. Using this Web service approach, the user was able to obtain access to a reader program that solved his or her content-viewing problem.

Note, however, that this particular Web service was provided without using UDDI to find an available service (instead, programmers hard-coded the location of the Web site that contained the readers). In this case, we saw two programs working cooperatively together (notice that the requester made a request to send a file-extension reader, and that a reader was ultimately sent).

Note also that this Web service application didn't use WSDL to negotiate how the service would be provided. And it's doubtful that SOAP protocol was used to bind the file transfer session—instead a simple command using TCP/IP's FTP protocol was probably used.

Additionally, observe that the service was provided "semiautomatically"—that is, user intervention had to take place to get the service that was originally requested. When all of the Web services protocols are used, this process can be designed to take place transparently; the user may not even be aware that a Web services program acted on his or her behalf to retrieve a reader program. The whole translation task can happen in the background with no user intervention.

The bottom line in this example is that a Web service was provided (as evidenced by two applications cooperating to provide the user with a service), but this service was not based on using Web services protocols or a UDDI registry. Hence, it is possible to receive Web services without using the formal Web services standards—but note also that using this approach can be somewhat manual rather than programmatic/automatic in nature.

**How This Application Would Work as a Truly Automated Web Service**

The following example describes how this program may ultimately work when implemented using formal Web services protocols and directory services:

SIDEBAR 3-2
## HOW THIS APPLICATION MAY SOME DAY WORK

- A requester application asks a UDDI directory to find a site that has a reader for a particular file extension;

- The UDDI directory contains a list of sites that have published the availability of such readers;

- The requester's WSDL application then steps-in to negotiate for the use of that reader (some readers are free, others are available on a chargeable basis);

- Once the business terms and conditions have been executed, WSDL turns over the rest of the transaction to SOAP. SOAP binds the communications session and the reader is sent to the user.

- And, if you want to get really fancy, that reader should be able to unpack itself, automatically read the previously unreadable content, and present that content for viewing to the user. And, all of this should be done transparently and instantaneously.

The big difference between the two examples is that the approach in the first one is highly manual in nature, while that in the second example—the formal Web standards-based approach—enables this format-conversion service to take place *automatically* and *transparently.*

Web service applications can be written without the use of Web services protocols and directories. Doing this, however, involves either manual user intervention to instruct the system how and where to obtain a Web service, or "hard-coding" in order to enable applications to find each other and work cooperatively together. User intervention defeats the purpose of Web services—it eliminates the "automatic and transparent" service provisioning aspect that Web services have been designed to deliver. And hard-coding defeats the ability of a Web-based application to search the Internet for other applications that may be better suited to the service purpose—again defeating fundamental aspects of Web services, such as finding the best service for the job or negotiating with other applications for the best service deal.

## Chapter Summary

In Chapter 2 you learned that Web services are standards that enable requester and service programs to *easily* find each other, agree on how to transfer information, and communicate with each other over the Internet. To be more specific, Web services are based on certain registry services and application program interfaces and on communications protocols that can help applications programs find each other (using UDDI); agree on how to communicate and share information (WSDL); complete the handshake with a "bound" communications session (using SOAP); and use HTTP protocol as a transport for Internet communications.

Also in Chapter 2 you learned how Web services are "supposed to" flow. You learned how requester applications request services and what the respective roles of UDDI, WSDL, and SOAP are in delivering XML-formatted data from a service application to a requester application.

This chapter gave you more in-depth information on Web services technologies—with a major focus on XML. You learned that XML represents a way to describe and share data using a common presentation format. You also learned that more than 900 XML schema are being used today— meaning that more than 900 "forms" are now being used by various industries to provide a common way to represent industry-specific data and information. You need to understand that representing data in XML form is nontrivial and  that much of the pioneering work needed to produce XML data for your particular industry may have already been done.

In this chapter you also learned that Web services are sometimes implemented without the use of UDDI, WSDL, and SOAP registry/directory services and protocols. This point is important, because most vendor write-ups and many news articles neglect to mention that other protocols and program-locator technologies are used in lieu of Web services in order to build many first-generation Web services prototype applications. Web services have tremendous potential to become the preferred method for applications to exchange data with one and other—but in the short term many early adopters are using other protocols or application-location services as supplements until Web services protocols mature a bit more.

The benefits of writing Web services applications *without* using Web services protocols are related to the following:

1. *Sophistication*—The level of sophistication of other approaches (COM, DCOM, CORBA, etc.) is often more mature in security, manageability, reliability, and other important "abilities" necessary for enterprise-class programming environments.

2. *Expediency*—Using existing code or other program-to-program architectures to pass XML data can be more expedient than rewriting applications using Web services protocols.

On the other hand, when Web services are implemented using other approaches, users may find the process to be less automated (more manual) than if the applications had been written using a formal Web services approach (the format-conversion application in this chapter illustrated this point). For instance, when UDDI is not used, developers are called upon to hard-code the location of Web services to be provided (meaning that an application developer has to put directions to a particular Web site into his/her code to direct the requester application to the service needed). The non-standards-based approaches can be more cumbersome for the programmer (and can create a situation where the programmer may have to maintain the code should the hard-coded application be changed) and less automated for the user.

In the short term it is reasonable to expect early-adopter enterprises to use existing application objects, other distributed computing architectures and APIs, and hard-coded directory functions to build their initial Web services implementations. As a result, these implementations will sometimes require manual intervention and hard-coding in order to find cooperative applications, or they may work only with applications that use the same "proprietary" APIs (like the DCOM example cited)—meaning that these applications will only be able to communicate with like systems.

In the longer term, in order for true, fully automated, transparent platform-independent, program-to-program communications to take place, applications will need to use common standards such as UDDI, WSDL, SOAP, HTTP, XML schema, and other standards and conventions.

# 4

# Gotchas

In This
Chapter:

- A discussion of some of the weak points of state-of-the-art Web services

Key Insights:

- Web services architecture is weak (at this juncture) in several areas that are vital for mission-critical applications such as reliability, security, and manageability.
- Standards committees, the open-source community, and vendors are addressing these shortcomings. As a result, I believe that Web services architecture can be deployed in mission critical computing environments today—if properly augmented with third-party products.

C hapter 3 provided additional technical details about various Web services protocols, the registry, and the XML format/language. It also alluded to the fact that many Web services applications are now being built using other protocols (like COM or CORBA) in lieu of WSDL or SOAP. The reason is that Web services are still, in some respects, immature for handling complex, reliable, secure transactional and computational tasks.

This chapter takes a look at some of the weak points of today's Web services architecture. Improvements, however, are being made on a daily basis, and all of the issues raised in this section are in the process of being overcome.

## Weak Points in Web Services Architecture

Although hundreds of Web services applications have been written (a good list can be found at www.xmethods.com), the Web services architecture can still be considered to be "in its infancy." The reason is that, although UDDI, WSDL, and SOAP do work as advertised, numerous improvements need to be made to UDDI registry service and related Web services protocols to "harden" them for use in business critical production environments.

In my new role as president of Bloor Research–North America, I recently published a report (Web Services Gotchas) that identifies eight "shortcomings" of Web services architecture that may impede the progress of Web services in enterprise-class computing environments (see Figure 4–1).

In short, at Bloor Research–North America we believe that there are certain Web services shortcomings that must be

| Security/Privacy |
| Messaging/Routing |
| Quality-of-Service/Reliability |
| Transaction Processing |
| Management |
| Performance |
| Interoperability |

FIGURE 4-1   Web Services Shortcomings/Gotchas According to Bloor Research. *Source:* Bloor Research–North America, May, 2002. Used by Permission.

overcome to foster the adoption of the architecture in message-rich, transaction-heavy, enterprise-class computing environments.

A closer look at the "gotchas" reveals the following shortcomings:

- *Security/privacy*—Specifically ensuring that content can be authenticated and validated, can restrict authorization rights to prevent unauthorized viewers from using restricted content, and that ways can be found to ensure data integrity.

- *Routing/messaging, Reliability/quality-of-service/transaction handling*—Protocols must be developed to track messages through multiple intermediaries. Standards must be established to ensure messaging reliability (this is especially important in financial transaction processing scenarios where the underlying Web services architecture must be capable of "rolling-back" transactions to their original state should a failure of some sort occur). Until these protocols are developed (or become more mature), Bloor Research will continue to identify these areas as shortcomings.

- *Transaction-handling in particular*—All preceding distributed computing architectures provided ways to monitor and track transactions, roll-back transactions, and manage/tune application and systems environments to ensure optimal performance. Many of these architectures made use of transaction monitors to accomplish this task. The W3C has not, and is not in the process, of creating a standard transaction monitor. Thus, this task will roll to vendors or open-source software providers. And at present, the lack of a robust Web services standard for transaction tracking/roll-back/monitoring is, in the opinion of Bloor Research–North America (NA), a Web services shortcoming.

- *Manageability*—The lack of an overall plan for managing Web services environments (from a system, network, and application level) makes Bloor Research NA consider Web services manageability an architectural shortcoming. (Note that many vendors are stepping forward with robust, Web services-capable frameworks and products to assist in Web services management in the short term as well as for the long term.)

- *Interoperability*—The formation of the WS-I goes a long way toward addressing Bloor Research NA's concern about how interoperability will be achieved across multiple disparate platforms and differing application program language environments. Still, the newness of the WS-I, plus its initial political positioning (leaving Sun off the invite list until the last minute), makes Bloor Research a little suspicious of the group's motivations. Hence, interoperability is identified as a shortcoming.

- *Performance/tuning*—There is a distinct lack of performance tuning information and/or tools for optimizing Web services computing environments. Although the W3C does internal quality assurance (and has even published some of its test suites/tuning utilities), it is Bloor Research NA's opinion that not enough is being done here to assure that Web services applications can be optimized to compete from a performance perspective with tightly coupled distributed computing architectures. Hence, we see performance/tuning as an exposure to the general acceptance of Web services architecture by enterprise clients—and thus consider performance/tuning to be a shortcoming.

In Bloor Research NA's opinion, the bottom line is that for Web services to be accepted at the enterprise level issues such as reliability, quality-of-service, transaction handling, security, manageability, and more must be addressed in a cohesive fashion. And the good news is that, through the efforts of the W3C, the vendor community, open-source software providers, and consortia, all of these shortcomings are being addressed.

**Having Stated This…**     Our latest research shoes that by mixing and matching Web services standards-based product with "enhancers" (other open-source or vendor-produced products that fill in the gaps in Web services architecture), reliable, secure Web services environments can be built. And, by using messaging appliances, performance tuning software, and other hardware and software products, performance-related issues can be overcome (or at least mitigated).

As a result of discussions with early-adopter Web services users and vendors, Bloor Research NA believes the following:

Even though Bloor Research NA has identified several Web services shortcomings that must be addresses by formal standards activity over time, it is our opinion that these shortcomings are not showstoppers, and we advise that enterprises not wait to experiment with and build Web services solutions. Between the advances being made within the W3C standards committees, and the advances and extensions being built by the open-source and vendor communities, very functional (even mission-critical) Web services environments can be built and deployed today.

We do observe that, at this juncture, Web services architecture is best deployed in-house (on a corporate intranet) or on a protected virtual private network (with known secure business partners) because HTTP-based Web services can leave open holes for external hacking/invasion to take place. We also believe that at this juncture, Web services routing/message handling (and transaction handling) is not well-suited for handling heavy transactional environments unless third-party products (like appliances that off-load message handling and perform security tasks) are used to augment simple Web services routing and messaging.

Still, by taking these issues into consideration (and by using workarounds to overcome these issues) there appears to be no need to wait several years until the standards mature before experimenting with Web services architecture. Web services architecture can be used successfully today in enterprise-class, production computing environments (provided it is properly augmented with the right mix of vendor-supplied hardware and software extensions to make it secure and reliable and capable of handling a lot of message traffic).

*Source:* Bloor Research–North America (Web Services Gotchas). Used by Permission.

## Chapter Summary

Many books on the subject of Web services tend to be overly optimistic—they overlook some of the shortcomings or challenges being faced by evolving Web services architecture.

There are, at this juncture, several obstacles that potential adopters should be aware of as they look to build and implement their own Web services implementations. There are also several work-arounds that can be used to get around Web services protocol, registry, security, reliability, and other shortcomings. Some of these work-arounds include:

- Hard-coding the location of applications so that applications know where to find each other (this was covered in Chapter 3).
- Using point products to fill in the gaps in Web services architecture (the Forum Systems secure XML Web services appliance is a good example of such an approach).
- Using "complete" Web services products (such as IBM's WebSphere platform discussed in Chapter 1) that fill in the Web services-gaps while also providing rich application development tools, business process management tools, and the like.

Today's Web services are robust enough to be used in mission-critical computing environments. But they need to be augmented with third-party products in order to be used in secure, reliable, highly transactional business situations. Fortunately, the tools and products needed to supplement and augment the shortcomings in Web services are currently available. (Many of these solutions are discussed in depth in the vendor selection chapter of this book.)

# part II

## An Idea/Strategic Planning Guide for Business Executives

# 5

What Do Web Services Enable My Organization to Do?

**Key Insights:**

- There are nine different ways (at least) to use Web services to help improve organizational efficiency, open new business opportunities, recreate supply/distribution chains, and otherwise reinvent existing business models. Generic examples of how Web services can be used are included in this chapter; real-world examples are provided in the next chapter.

**P**revious chapters have provided you with an understanding of how Web services work and have described some issues, as well as work-arounds that can enable your organization to overcome certain Web services shortcomings. Now it's time to explore what Web services can enable you to do.

Web services fundamentally change the way that information systems can be built. Applications can be assembled on-the-fly; they can work across multiple systems architectures; and/or they can be deployed across various internal and external systems. No matter which approach or combination of approaches an enterprise chooses, the biggest paybacks generally are that (1) businesses can reduce costs related to application development; (2) businesses can respond more quickly to market or competitive changes; and (3) businesses can increase operational efficiency (through business integration of Web-based applications).

Over time, Web services will be used to change the entire business and go-to-market strategies of a wide range of enterprises. Web services applications will be used to change the way enterprises position themselves, the services they provide to customers, and the way that they work with business partners and other members of their supply chains. Further, Web services will allow companies to bring their unique software to market, thus opening opportunities to remarket existing intellectual content in new and different ways.

In the Executive Summary chapter, I identified nine separate and distinct ways to use Web services for strategic advantage (these are repeated in Figure 5–1). This chapter examines each of these points from a strategic "what's possible to do" perspective, such that business executives can understand the strategic ramifications of Web services to their existing and future business models.

### Nine Reasons to Embrace Web Services Architecture

1. Rapidly open new markets
2. Create new organizational efficiencies
3. Reduce application development costs
4. Create/overcome competitive pressure
5. Create new sources of revenue using existing intellectual capital
6. Repackage existing products to better reach/serve existing markets
7. Solve systems inoperability problems
8. Dynamically grow an existing applications portfolio
9. Increase/improve organizational and individual productivity

FIGURE 5-1   Web Services Benefits.

# Web Services in Action: Generic Examples

To illustrate how Web services will be used to accomplish these various objectives, this chapter uses "big picture" theoretical examples of how Web services can be implemented in order to illustrate what Web services-based applications are capable of doing. Subsequent chapters focus on these same elements using anecdotes and examples of how real-world Web services applications developers are building Web services-enabled applications today.

# How Web Services Can Help a Business Open New Markets

Let's say that your company runs a worldwide auto parts distribution business. You have basic run-the-business applications (financial payment systems, sales, distribution, inventory, etc.) and may have implemented a business-to-business transaction system that links your inventory and shipping department to a transportation company that delivers your orders.

Using today's *non-Web services model*, your company as part of its core inventory and distribution system will likely have "hard-coded" information about your transporter's method of doing business, its terms and conditions, its shipping and delivery charges, its delivery schedules, and more into a database that helps integrate your core system with your external shipper.

Now, just suppose that your company wants to expand—shipping parts to countries that its transporter does not cover. Now someone will have to contact new transporters, structure new business agreements, and send contracts out for competitive bid—right?

Not with Web services. With Web services your core application can be instructed to find other applications that can provide services to the core application. In this case, a wealth of companies capable of delivering your products to prospective customers may exist in a Web services UDDI directory. Those transporters will have listed characteristics about their companies—and how your company can do business with them. Payment and delivery terms will have been automated, and potentially even a parts tracking system may be active (courtesy of another Web services provider). The whole process of establishing a business relationship that allows transporters to distribute your products globally can thus be automated.

As a result of using Web services, the inability of your established transporter to deliver your products to your customers should no longer cause your business to be geographically restricted. By using Web services, applications are able to automatically find other, alternative transporters capable of delivering your products (even potentially at a lower cost)—thus improving your company's geographic reach and potentially increasing its overall profitability.

In this scenario, Web services allowed your company to expand into new markets by automatically and dynamically finding other "service" programs to help your company expand its global reach.

By using Web services standards that enable applications to work cooperatively over the Internet and by paying careful attention to how work and information flows between "requesters" (humans or applications) and Web services providers (Web services applications and databases), this automotive parts company can integrate its software applications with those of its partners and suppliers and thus expand its market reach while improving overall efficiency in the supply chain (which, in turn, results in more profitable business operations). In short, using Web services to automate functions and streamline processes helped this automotive company open new markets for its products.

**Not So Fast...**    Now for a dose of reality. The aforementioned example is "theoretically possible." But in reality the UDDI registry needed to enable this auto parts company to find other distributors and to programmatically establish distributor relationships with its new business partners does not yet exist.

Public UDDI directories are just now being assembled—led by companies like IBM, NTT, Microsoft, HP, and SAP that want to encourage the formation of large, public directories of Web services-based applications.

Meanwhile, small "private" UDDI directories are starting to sprout up. These directories are designed to service the needs of smaller communities of Web services users—for instance, users who are trying to establish healthcare, insurance, or other "vertical market" specialized Web services environments, or even auto parts distributors as illustrated earlier. (The InterPro Global Partners example used later on in this book is also a good example of a specialized Web services community.)

Be aware that despite the absence of a rich industry directory of available Web services, Web services applications can still be written. Humans need to intervene to tell Web services applications where to look for the services that they require, however, rather than applications being able to automatically look up the location of cooperative applications in a UDDI directory. This is how most Web services applications are being written today.

Despite the lack of a generalized public-domain UDDI directory, this auto parts example is important because (1) it shows how Web services can ultimately work and (2) it sets the proper expectation for business managers about how mature the Web services standards really are.

## How Web Services Can Be Used to Dynamically Increase a Company's Application Portfolio

Throughout the 1990s and into the 21st century, businesses have been struggling to integrate "packaged" applications into their overall enterprise application portfolios. (A packaged application is one that has been purchased "off the shelf" from an independent software vendor to run some business function.) Typically today's enterprises are struggling to implement and customize the following:

- Enterprise Resource Planning (ERP) applications (which run a company's financial, human resource, sales, manufacturing, distribution, and other inward-looking applications).

- Customer Resource Management (CRM) applications (which run customer services, sales-force automation, and other outward-looking functions).
- Supply Chain Management (SCM) applications (which streamline a company's interaction with its supply-chain partners).

Among the many tasks involved in implementing these packages are customizing code for an enterprise's particular needs and performing integration among all three of these applications (such that CRM sales-force applications can provide feedback to ERP sales and manufacturing systems, for instance). Building highly integrated ERP/CRM/SCM applications can be extremely complex, time consuming, and costly.

Now, imagine a scenario where all of these "packaged" applications suddenly become available as services on the Web. Imagine that an enterprise could pick the suite of ERP applications desired and that those applications could work automatically with CRM or SCM applications (because all three could use UDDI directories, WSDL protocols, and SOAP protocols to communicate and share data and information). Web services creates just such an environment by creating standards that enable applications to present data in common and consistent ways and by providing protocols for applications to negotiate how to share such information and at what cost.

Using a Web services approach, enterprises will some day be able to dynamically assemble application portfolios that meet their particular computing needs while avoiding much of the expensive integration and deployment expense related to designing, deploying, and managing ERP, CRM, and SCM applications. On the flip side of this coin, hundreds if not thousands of software suppliers will change their approach to market: instead of focusing on selling package licenses, these software makers will focus on selling applications as services (and charge a subscription fee for so doing).

Figure 5–2 illustrates how businesses can use Web services to dynamically build an application portfolio. It also articulates a few of the benefits derived by moving to a Web services application model.

## Portfolio Development Today

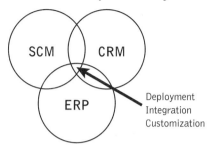

### Today's Challenges

- Purchase, deploy, and integrate ERP, CRM, and SCM applications
- Modify software packages to adapt them to your specific business needs
- Perform additional work to integrate packaged software with other packaged software (for instance, integrating CRM systems with ERP financial systems)
- Modify business processes
- Confront the problem that custom code development is expensive and time consuming (delays could lose market window)

## Portfolio Development Tomorrow

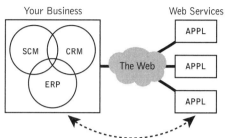

Easy integration using Web standards, business process management, and well-integrated Web infrastructure server

### Tomorrow's Opportunities

- Dynamically capture/integrate other application/ transaction environments to suit your company's application needs and expand your company's service offerings (barter or pay a transaction fee for such services)
- Use business process management software to allow for further streamlining of business processes (efficiency)
- Reduce expenditures for custom code development (can use applications invented elsewhere)

### Advantages of Web Services

- Streamlined business operations increase productivity
- Reduced cost of operations directly affects the company's bottom line
- New model allows executive management to expand business in new directions by using other people's applications and services to create competitive advantage

FIGURE 5-2   Dynamic Application Portfolio Development: Challenges and Opportunities.

**Not So Fast...**   For this scenario to become a reality, much work has to be done in building public UDDI directories; and much work has to be done by ISVs in writing WSDL templates that allow for application interoperability as well as data/information sharing.

Still, it is important to note that solid progress is being shown in the creation of Web services UDDI registries. The following SAP press release illustrates this point.

**WALLDORF, Germany—October 4, 2001** SAP AG (NYSE: SAP), the world's leading provider of e-business software solutions, today announced it has become a global UDDI Operator and will build on UDDI for service integration and publish global services within the UDDI Business Registry. With this threefold strategy, SAP will fully leverage UDDI for e-business solutions—from providing SAP® functionality for Web services to using services published through UDDI. This strategy will provide SAP customers with an easy path to participate in and drive collaborative business.

The Universal Description, Discovery and Integration (UDDI) Business Registry is a global, public, online directory that gives businesses a uniform way to describe their services, discover other companies' services, and understand the methods necessary to conduct e-business with a particular company. As a key element of the framework that makes Web services a reality, the UDDI Business Registry is an implementation based on the UDDI Specifications, which are available at www.uddi.org/.

"SAP is focused on developing solutions that break down technical barriers and help companies transact business on a global level," said Karl-Heinz Hess, member of the extended executive board of SAP AG. "With SAP fully embracing UDDI, SAP customers will receive all the technology infrastructure and services to develop, deploy and manage Web services, which supports SAP's position as the leading e-business solution provider."

As part of becoming a UDDI Business Registry Operator, SAP will build, run and maintain a global UDDI node, enabling businesses to register and discover Web services via the Internet. SAP has been a driving member of the UDDI initiative, which enables businesses to quickly, easily and dynamically collaborate, since its inception.

"We are pleased with SAP's continued support of the UDDI initiative by its joining the UDDI Business Registry Operators, Microsoft, IBM and Hewlett-Packard, in hosting a public UDDI Business Registry for Web services, as well as through product integration," said Tom Glover, general program manager for uddi.org. "With UDDI, companies of all sizes can register themselves to gain exposure to other e-businesses looking for specific B2B relationships. SAP is truly preparing its customers to take advantage of Web services by using UDDI for services publishing and integration."

SAP will make it possible to provide the application functions of the mySAP.com® e-business platform as a service, which makes it easy for customers to provide this information externally through UDDI. In addition, SAP customers can use UDDI to quickly and easily find and integrate complementary services regardless of their location. For example, a service such as "check product availability" can be performed without putting the integration challenge on the IT manager…

SAP customers can register their business through the SAP Service Marketplace. At the customer's request, the stored business information can be published in the UDDI Business Registry, made available globally and enhanced by individual services. SAP has already registered itself and started to publish its global services offerings, such as the "test drive" of the mySAP.com e-business platform, in UDDI.
*Source*: http://www.sap.com/press/press.asp?pressID=629. Used by Permission.

Notice in this article that Microsoft, IBM, Hewlett-Packard, and now SAP are all building common UDDI directory services such that applications can use Web services to find cooperative service applications. All of these companies clearly believe that Web services represent a viable way to create large registries of sharable applications and have taken the steps necessary to help jump-start the industry in order to build such UDDI registries. With this vendor line up, and with over 500 vendors committed to helping build Web services standards (as part of the W3C consortium), it is reasonable to conclude that Web services will become a viable standard for cross-platform program-to-program communications.

## How Web Services Can Be Used to Reduce Development Time and Costs

This example—a hypothetical banking environment—illustrates how Web services can be used to reduce programming time and costs, thus enabling the bank to bring new banking products to market more quickly.

A bank may have a core application that provides its customers with information on their savings and checking accounts. But the bank may also wish to provide loan, mortgage, life insurance, or other additional services to its customers in order to increase its revenue stream. The traditional way of adding these services has been either to build custom applications that offer such services or to locate packaged applications and then manually integrate those applications with the bank's core application. In applications developer's terms, the new applications would be "bolted on" to the existing application.

By using Web services standards the new applications that the bank wishes to add can be found on the Web and easily integrated into the bank's existing application portfolio, thus reducing the time to develop custom applications and the related costs for development and integration work. By using XML as the basic content format and making use of Web services standards such as UDDI, WSDL, and SOAP, the bank can quickly find new applications (services) and integrate them in a dynamic and fluid fashion with its existing application portfolio (see Figure 5–3).

**The Practice Today**

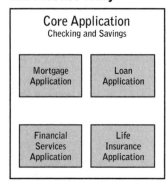

Banks usually build their own or acquire loan, mortgage, life insurance, and financial services software, then laboriously integrate that software with the core.

**Dynamic e-Business Web Services**

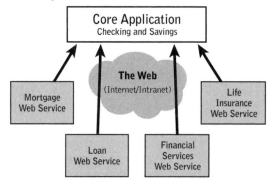

Banks can now look elsewhere on the Internet to augment their core application portfolio. The new Web services application can be easily integrated with existing applications using newly evolved Web standards. Conversely, banks can resell home-grown applications to create a new revenue source.

FIGURE 5-3    Hypothetical Banking Use of Web Services.

Note in Figure 5–3 that the bank used Web services to find, build, test, integrate, and deploy Web-based application services. Essentially the bank was able to reach out over the Web, find application modules that could satisfy its needs, and rapidly integrate those products within the existing bank infrastructure. In this case, the bank didn't have to worry about what platform, operating system, or programming language was used by the Web services application module—it all just worked, because the bank and the service module provider made use of the same format (XML) and the same Web services standards (UDDI, WSDL, and SOAP).

This example illustrates how time-to-develop and time-to-market can be reduced using Web services standards to find and bind new applications into the bank's existing portfolio.

Also worthy of note is that Web services focus largely on processes and less on programming. Application developers and programmers will be able to publish their applications location and specifications using UDDI and WSDL, and then the real magic happens when business-level people and consumers start to string together webs of services that they need in order to accomplish their respective goals. In other words, Web services enables less technical people to link together various services, creating a whole new application-development approach to business and consumer problem solving. In the case of Web services, the solutions that people string together are what deliver value—the actual programming is the means to the end.

Also, observe that the people who are linking various applications together to deliver business or consumer value are often nontechnical (and this is significant in terms of the cost to develop applications). Using less technically skilled individuals to create value chains of Web services applications represents an opportunity to save huge sums of money within enterprises.

**Not So Fast...** Again, we must acknowledge that finding new Web-enabled applications on the Web is somewhat difficult today, owing to the lack of an expansive UDDI directory service. However, after programmers hard-code the links to the desired new Web-based applications (or after users make manual choices in order to find and use the Web services that they desire), the rest of this banking application is entirely "doable" using today's state-of-the-art Web services standards.

## How Web Services Can Help Create New Organizational Efficiencies

Note in the previous example how the bank was able to use Web services to create process flow efficiencies (usually translating into reduced sales, general, and administrative costs and greater organizational profitability).

Business process management enables enterprises to establish policies (for instance, who can use what applications under what conditions) and procedures (how applications are to interact) and to organize workflow (optimize the order in which applications are executed to eliminate redundancy and speed up processing). By properly designing the ebb-and-flow of business processes, a well-organized enterprise can create great efficiencies. In the preceding example, by using Web services this bank was able to quickly add new products to its portfolio (making the bank more competitive and increasing the chances for additional profit). And this bank has the opportunity to further streamline its operations by using business process management software to integrate its various Web services applications with its traditional core applications—thus improving internal efficiency by breaking down internal organizational barriers while also improving the customer experience.

What is missing from the banking example is consideration of business process flow. To make the most efficient use of its new Web services-based applications, the bank must also find a way to improve the process flow of information within the bank and to its customers.

For instance, it would be great for a bank to help a customer ascertain whether he or she was qualified for a mortgage, but shouldn't the bank at the same time be able to present that customer with information about the bank's current loan rates and terms? And shouldn't the bank make it easy for the customer to "sign on the dotted-line" for that mortgage immediately? And, if the customer signs up, shouldn't other bank systems be made aware that he or she has become a mortgage customer and could also be a prospect for financial planning or life insurance services?

To make this happen, the new Web services applications would need to be integrated with other traditional banking applications as well as with the bank's workflow processes. The bank would than have access to new business opportunities as well as experience new efficiencies (because various applications would be working together to solve customer problems rather than working across departmental or organizational business unit lines). The resulting opportunities to garner new sources of revenue combined with cross-organizational efficiency would be passed directly to the bank's bottom line in terms of reduced sales/ general/administrative (SG&A) costs.

At present there are no formal standards for business rules and business process management. Instead, builders of Web services need to augment their Web services architecture with a "rules engine" or business process management software that deals with how to optimize workflow and processes. For IT and business managers there are dozens of rules engines, workflow products, and business process management software packages on the market today from which to choose. And several vendors are working to closely integrate their business process management tools with their respective Web services offerings.

Some Web services product suites that include tools to simplify application development and automate business process flow are offered by:

- BEA (with its WebLogic servers);
- IBM (with its WebSphere Personalization Server and/ or related business-rule "beans");
- Microsoft (with its BizTalk software environment); and
- Hewlett-Packard, Oracle, and others.

These suppliers and their product lines are covered in greater depth in the comparative/competitive section later in this book. Note that all of these products have extensions (software not directly related to Web services standards) enabling enterprises to establish policies and procedures that allow for efficient process and workflow between Web-based applications.

## How Web Services Can Help an Enterprise Create/Overcome Competitive Pressure

Web services provide enterprises with a double-edged sword. Early-adopter enterprises will be able to exploit existing Web services applications to gain competitive edge while later adopters will be able to make use of Web services to respond more quickly than ever before to competitive threats and pressures. Thus, in one case, Web services can be used as an offensive tool—and in the other, Web services can come to the rescue as a defensive tool.

The next example portrays competition between two independent software vendors in the Professional Services Automation (PSA) marketplace. For those not familiar with this marketplace, we begin with a quick overview:

All Professional Services Organizations (PSOs)—whether they be dedicated management/IT consultancies, law firms, internal IT departments, architectural/engineering firms, media publishing, research and development, or government organizations—base their businesses on providing/selling professional expertise and "billable time" worked on projects. Profit is derived by subtracting the cost of doing business (salary, travel and expense, sales/general/administrative support, benefits,…) from the amount of billable time accrued on strategic or tactical consulting/development projects. *Any activity that reduces nonbillable time or that reduces sales, general, and administrative (SG&A) costs increases the profitability of a PSO.*

This is where *Professional Services Automation* comes in. PSA software automates numerous PSO business processes and activities such as:

- Time, travel, and expense reporting (and PSA software links these applications to run-the-business, back-end reporting systems such as an organization's finance and human resource systems)

- Opportunity Management—Business/account development (customer/prospect sales opportunity development and tracking; automated proposal response)

- Program/Project Management (including quality controls)

- Resource Management—the scheduling of people resources (ensuring that the right people with the right skill levels are made available for the right jobs). Also, PSA affords managers the ability to generate a variety of reports that can help a

PSO use its people more efficiently and effectively by enabling managers to automatically create reports that provide the status of projects or track the availability of people resources for new projects

- Collaborative Processes—such that project workers, business partners, and clients can easily share information and work collaboratively toward project completion

- Knowledge Management (providing a centralized data repository and needed access and collaboration software to ensure that valuable experiential information is shared throughout the organization)

- Customer Relationship Management (CRM)—PSA can be integrated with traditional CRM software to ensure that customers have an adequate feedback mechanism to/from their PSA software supplier (includes call center support); to automate various aspects of the sales process; and to provide a PSO with the ability to design and deliver more effective marketing campaigns, lead management, tracking, and other customer development activities).

The bottom line: by automating manual and cumbersome processes that burn valuable professional time, PSOs can deliver more billable services to their clients and thus increase overall profitability. PSA software helps reduce sales, general, and administrative costs—enabling organizations to use professionals more efficiently and profitably.

Now that you have a basic understanding of how the PSA marketplace works, let's take a look at how two competitors could use Web services to expand their product sets in order to create competitive pressure and/or respond to competitive pressure. In the example illustrated in Figure 5–4, two PSA companies make use of third-party Web services application suppliers to augment and expand their respective product offerings. Step 1 shows ISV "A" adding a project management services that enables it to compete directly with ISV "B". In step 2, ISV B responds by adding a Time and Attendance service (enabling it to directly compete with ISV A) and On-line Analytical Processing (step 3)—responding to the original competitive threat and raising the bar for competition by adding a new capability to its product offering. Step 4 shows ISV A adding On-line Analytical Processing, thus creating parity between the two ISVs. But step 5 shows ISV B on the offensive, adding two

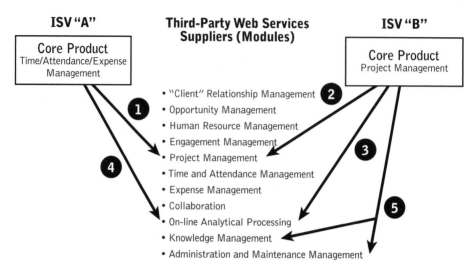

**FIGURE 5-4**    Creating/Overcoming Competitive Pressures Using the Web Services Model.

new features to its offering. This competition can go on ad infinitum (or at least until there are no new Web services to be added in order to compete in the PSA marketplace).

It is very important for business executives to understand the model illustrated in Figure 5–4. Let us look at what is actually happening:

- The third-party services are application "objects" that can be wedded to, and extend the functionality of, the ISV's core products. These modules can be fluid in nature (they can come and go as intermittent services) or they can be hard-wired to the core application and made always available. The vendors choose how they will offer the new service; the customers choose vendors that provide the payment terms they desired.

- The requester application and the service application negotiate the kind of service desired, the price, and other terms and conditions—while the customer sees nothing other than a new service being provided. This negotiation implies that the ISV and the third party either reach an agreement in person on how compensation will take place for the service or put instructions for that negotiation in the WSDL code used by each software package, and the two software products negotiate the terms and conditions for service provisioning.

By using this Web services model, ISVs (or end-user enterprises) can realize two distinct benefits: (1) they can assemble applications quickly in order to respond to competitive pressure or to take competitive advantage; and (2) the programmatic negotiation of business terms for services can greatly reduce administrative costs between software suppliers—reducing people and administrative overhead related to Web services provisioning. Accordingly, ISVs and enterprises can save money by reducing people costs related to contract negotiation and payment structuring/monitoring.

The argument that Web services can help an organization create or overcome competitive pressure rests on the fact that Web services enable competitors to "assemble" applications in new and different ways. This assemblage model enables them to quickly and flexibly create new go-to-market applications by using application "objects" to assemble "compound" applications.

**Not So Fast...**    Like previous examples, this ISV example relies on the availability of a UDDI directory to find Web services. And it relies on a fairly sophisticated use of WSDL to negotiate the business terms and compensation method to provide the Web service to the original requester. As part of this negotiation, micro-payments (small payments for services rendered) may apply. Finally, because these are "run-the-company" vital applications, neither the service providers nor their customers can afford to take chances with the reliability or security of the transactions that take place between requester and service applications.

The above scenario could work if the Web services described were structured so that they didn't make strict use of the official Web services protocols or methods—for instance,

- If the ISV and the third-party Web service solutions provider were to hard-code their application locations (then they could work around having to use UDDI).

- If people were to actually get involved in structuring the business arrangements, rather than relying on WSDL to do so (programs could be written to track the use of the service as well as to bill the requester accordingly).

- If security were augmented by a "plug-in" security package, such as industry-standard Kerberos or Public Key Infrastructure security methods.

- If a reliable network and system infrastructure could be constructed (for instance, a virtual private network to ensure reliable and secure transactions).

As you can see from this example, Web services hold great potential to automate program-to-program communications, but several shortcomings must be overcome. Note that for every shortcoming there is a potential work-around that would allow an enterprise or ISV to use Web services today to build such solutions. These work-arounds tend to be manual in nature. Over time, though, Web services standards will mature, and all of the services described above can be made automatic.

## How Web Services Can Help Create a New Revenue Stream from Existing Intellectual Property

Imagine the following scenario:

Your enterprise specializes in providing financial services for its customers. Your company has written six very distinct financial analysis and measurement, portfolio management, asset tracking, trend calculation software, and other financial service packages. Your company believes that three of these software solutions are strategic and should not be shared. By the same token, the other three offer strong value to your customers—and other financial services firms would be happy to pay your company for the use of them to improve their respective services offerings to their clients.

In this scenario your company has intellectual assets in the form of software. Some of those assets are strategic, while others could be remarketed to competitors or other organizations, thus augmenting their respective application portfolios. Instead of just leaving them locked behind your organization's closed doors, modifying those intellectual assets to be Web service compliant might open up a new source of revenue without creating any strategic or competitive threats—while incurring only small costs for the redesign of the product (into a Web services offering) and small long-term costs for the management and administration of the product. *Voila*—the use of Web services architecture has enabled your company to take advantage of underutilized intellectual capital to realize an instant revenue increase without tremendous capital or human resource investment!

**Not So Fast...** Although this scenario is entirely possible and can be achieved using Web services, you'll need to ask yourself the following questions:

1. How are my competitors and potential users going to find out about the availability of my newly Web-services-enabled services?
2. Will my competitors require that additional work be done to integrate the service being provided with their own internal applications portfolio?
3. How will my competitors feel about providing possibly sensitive account information to my Web service so that my applications can provide some sort of transactional or computational service for the requester application?

As in previous examples, the lack of a UDDI directory makes it difficult for Web services to be found. This example also illustrates new problems, such as how the sharing of account sensitive information can be securely accomplished.

Again, the lack of maturity in Web services standards prevents this kind of scenario from being accomplished in an automated fashion. Yet, it is still possible to architect such a solution by hard-coding applications together and rolling in add-on secure messaging facilities.

## How Web Services Can Help ISVs Repackage Their Software Offerings to Better Reach/Serve Existing Markets

Imagine a scenario where your company is late to market, is losing market share, or is unable to get customers to adopt your product solution because it would require the involvement of the Information Systems (IS) department for installation and management (and the IS group is already overburdened with other projects). What would happen if you repackaged your product as a Web service that required no IS involvement in design, installation, or management of your product offering? Could you then broaden the appeal of your product set?

Web services architecture allows for such repackaging, making it possible for software vendors to restructure the way they sell their products as well as providing new avenues to go-to-market. Using a Web services go-to-market approach, software makers can structure a new business model that enables them to approach target markets more efficiently than by using today's "traditional" approach. These efficiencies manifest themselves in faster time-to-market, lower promotional costs, and lower sales/general/administrative (SG&A) costs, and thereby contributing to a software maker's bottom-line profitability.

## Repacking Affects Physical Product Packaging, Marketing/Promotion, Business Partnership Strategies, and Sales-Channel Approaches

Figure 5–5 contrasts the traditional approach to product packaging, promotion, partnership development, and sales-channel strategies with the repackaging of products using a Web services approach.

As illustrated in Figure 5–5, the traditional approach is inherently cost intensive—largely because it involves too much investment capital to manufacture and promote a product, too much administrative overhead to structure business partner and customer relationships, too much time and effort to build a direct sales force, and/or too much

## Traditional Approach

### Build and Package Product

- Software maker designs and builds product
- Software maker physically packages software for sale to end-user organizations
- Involves manufacturing and distribution

### Marketing/Promotion

- Software maker puts together press/analyst plan in order to bring attention to product
- Advertising
- Can involve significant promotional $$$

### Business Partnerships

- Software maker may choose to find business partners to help bring product to market
- People/administrative/contract intensive

### Sales Channels

- Go-to-market is usually through direct sales force or by leveraging partner's sales force
- Direct is expensive; partners take margin...

## New, Web Services Approach

### Build and Package Product

- Software maker designs and builds product
- Software maker packages product as a hosted service (no need to manufacture or distribute)
- Result: significant cost reduction

### Marketing/Promotion

- Software maker uses UDDI directories to make other applications aware of services available
- UDDI can save the software maker from having to spend $$$ for extensive advertising

### Business Partnerships

- Software maker uses WSDL to automatically negotiate contracts and services
- Reduces administrative/contract costs

### Sales Channels

- Go-to-market does not require indirect or direct sales force
- Saves expense; faster time-to-market

FIGURE 5-5    Traditional Go-to-Market versus New Web Services Approach.

margin give-away to incent an indirect sales force to promote a given software product.

The traditional approach to building and packaging software involves the physical manufacture and distribution of the software package, which can be quite expensive. The Web services approach merely requires that the software maker "host" the application as a service on computers that their company (or a close business partner) run for Web-based clients. By packaging a software product for distribution over the Web, very significant costs for manufacturing and shipping can be avoided. This could make the Web services approach highly attractive to new software companies as well as those looking to reduce operating costs.

The traditional approach to marketing software products also involves creating product awareness and seeking/getting publicity. This is accomplished by chasing the press and analyst communities for attention and by investing (sometimes heavily) in advertising. Using the Web services model, a software maker can make its products "known" by publishing a description of them in a UDDI directory, where hundreds or thousands of people or programs may find them. This approach can greatly reduce expenditures on press/analyst activities as well as on traditional advertising.

Another efficiency that Web services could offer the software industry is in the area of structuring business partner and customer relationships. Currently, the approach to structuring business partnerships involves:

- using sales and technical people to search for potential partner prospects;
- then using legal advisors to structure a mutually agreeable business relationship; and
- then using other people to build and manage joint marketing efforts.

This traditional approach is both people- and process-intensive, as well as extremely costly. Using a Web services approach, applications would be able to describe what they can do, how they can link to a requester application, what the legal and financial terms are for doing business, and even how to resolve problems (problem escalation). Suddenly, the people- and cost-intensive traditional approach starts to look very unattractive in contrast to the efficient and cost-saving Web services approach to managing partner and customer relationships!

Finally, Figure 5–5 also shows that Web services can help software companies move their products to market more quickly and less expensively than by traditional approaches (because by listing a product in a UDDI directory they may not need to build a large direct or indirect sales force or even use a direct or indirect or indirect sales channel).

These benefits are related to listing products in a global UDDI directory. The logic is that UDDI directories will some day make products automatically known on a global basis to human or programmatic requesters of services. The need for a large sales force (which is expensive to build and maintain) or an indirect sales force (which can cost a software maker a significant amount of profit margin) to "push" a product to market can be obviated by making the product generally known and able to "sell itself," using WSDL to describe itself to interested requester programs.

**Not So Fast...** It is reasonable to expect that over time a majority of software makers will embrace this Web services oriented business model. After all, it greatly reduces operating expenses related to sales/general/administrative costs; it reduces the need to spend vast sums of money on advertising and promotion; and it reduces the need to use human labor in structuring business and customer relationships.

But for this to occur, UDDI directories will have to become more prevalent and WSDL templates more robust in the way that they automate business negotiation functions. In short, the "publish/find/and bind" functions of Web services environments will need to become more sophisticated in order to enable the "new Web-services approach" described above to become a reality.

## How Web Services Can Help Solve Legacy Systems Incompatibility Problems

Imagine the following scenarios:

1. Your company (or government) decides that it wants to provide its customers (constituents) with a slew of new services over the Internet. However, the services needed reside on legacy (aged) systems that run nonmainstream operating environments and are written in nonmainstream development languages.

2. Your company acquires a competitor that happens to use a completely different systems infrastructure. (You use mainframe hardware and Cobol or Fortran programming languages; they use Windows platforms for operations and the C++ language for application development.)

In the past, either of these scenarios might have meant great gnashing of teeth for IS managers. The need to mesh disparate systems and network infrastructure, applications environments, and databases usually led to:

- One of the systems environments being chosen as the "standard" while the other was either jettisoned or eventually phased out);
- Complete systems retraining for individuals who were on the losing side of the system standard choice; and
- Lots of additional work integrating disparate databases and applications.

Today, at least the communications highway that each company (or the government) used would be consistent; they would use the TCP/IP communications protocol, which is the basis for Internet communications. On this common basis Web services can provide a solution for system-to-system, program-to-program interoperability.

Web services enable applications written in different languages to present their data in a common form (XML) to each other. And the common information highway, the Internet, makes it possible for these two environments to share data. By setting up a private UDDI directory, Web services enabled applications could find each other and share information. And by using SOAP, sessions can be bound between these disparate computing environments. Thus, through the use of Web services protocols and registry services, disparate applications and databases can be made to work together without the total redesign of systems, application, and database that might have been necessary in days gone by.

In the scenario where the government provides services to external constituents, notice in Figure 5–6 how a user can make a request over the Internet for a service—and how the UNIX/Java system calls the legacy system for data. Once it receives that data, the information/service is provided back to the constituent transparently. (The recipient receives a service made possible by using Web services architecture between two disparate system types behind the Internet cloud.)

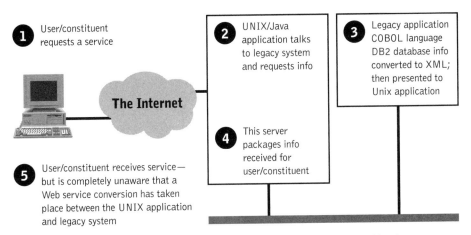

FIGURE 5-6    Web Services on the Back End to Help Resolve System/Data/Application
Incompatibilities.

**Not So Fast...**    A lot of work has gone into making Web services easy to use for those who program in the C++, C#, or Java application development languages. Many application development environments have been optimized to enable C or Java code to be automatically compiled (converted into efficient system code), and many vendors offer code that assists in the automation of workflow among applications. Such is not the case, however, for less mainstream languages such as Fortran, Cobol, and several other once popular or somewhat specialized languages. Hence, the real state of the art in terms of cross-environment language support is geared for C-based or Java-based language environments.

Note that in our example scenarios the lack of a common, public UDDI directory was not a factor, because each scenario needed to provide Web services only to internal applications. (In other words, hard-coding the location of the applications that share services is a perfectly acceptable practice in these scenarios.)

## Another Example of How Web Services Can Help Resolve Interoperability Issues

Imagine a scenario where (1) an enterprise has several packaged or custom applications that contain data needed to create a specialized report, (2) each of these "back-end" applications has the capability of formatting and presenting that data in XML format, and (3) each could also communicate with a decision-support application using WSDL. In this scenario, Web services could be used to resolve communications issues related to sharing data as well as communicating data between diverse application environments.

Let's take a closer look:

WSDL enables applications to work cooperatively together, regardless of what hardware, operating environment, or programming language each application uses. For example, WSDL can be used as an intermediary for a decision-support application to access data held within disparate back-end application environments (for instance, XML data that is held in PeopleSoft, SAP, or custom application files). In this case, a decision-support application could ask WSDL to negotiate the interface to various back-end application programs in order to gain access to XML data. WSDL would then request the appropriate data from various back-end sources and return that data in a common readable form to the decision-support application (see Figure 5–7), which could easily process it.

It is reasonable to expect that more and more enterprises will start to use WSDL services to help integrate XML data from various application sources, because WSDL helps solve complex application integration issues. In the present example, not only are disparate applications able to communicate data, but end users are also able to automatically compile reports without having to have specialized applications created to access information that resides in differing application environments. (This saves time, increases productivity, and reduces custom development costs.) This use of Web services has real business benefit, enabling an enterprise to achieve new efficiencies (because gathering information is less manual and far easier than when using multiple interfaces to disparate applications).

*Source*: Intel Corporation: The Spider's Web; http://cedar.intel.com (Intel Developer Services). Copyright © 2002 Intel Corporation. Used with Permission.

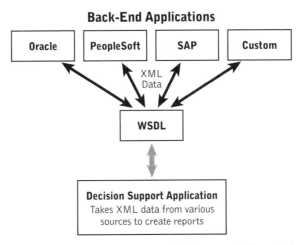

FIGURE 5-7   WSDL Used to Enable Interoperability with Legacy, Packaged, and Custom Applications.

## How Web Services Improve Individual Productivity

All of the previous generic examples focused on how Web services could be applied to businesses to improve productivity (through better business process flow), reduce costs (by easier, more efficient programming), and react to changing market/competitive conditions and other business-focused scenarios. But Web services can be built to serve the needs of individuals as well as businesses.

Imagine a scenario where you are willing to receive messages at any time or in any place from only a few select individuals. For instance, you may wish to allow such transmissions from your wife or husband, your mom, or selected business partners or associates. Currently, you can wear a pager—a dedicated device that allows you to receive messages. But those messages can be from anyone, not only from your selected people. Plus, pagers don't work in some locations—for instance, 30,000 feet up when you're in a plane. And you may not own a pager.

Along come "personalizable" Web services applications—application programs that can be instructed to deliver messages from people or programs that you have indicated to any Internet-enabled device you designate. The basic concept is that you have access to a Web service program that acts as your personal assistant or personal valet. This program can be made aware of your preferences and can deliver specified types of information to whatever Internet-enabled device you choose. In the aforementioned scenario, you may have instructed your personal Web services program to deliver messages from a select group of people to you via e-mail only between the hours of 9:00 a.m. and 1 p.m. (because you expect to be on a flight between those hours and you plan to be using the Internet and your e-mail system on the plane). Or you may have instructed a stock program to notify you of a particular change in your portfolio. In each case your personal Web service can be instructed to carry out your desires.

Notice in this example that a UDDI registry was not necessary in order to provide these services. Further, the role of WSDL in negotiating the service was minimal—the applications were simply taking messages delivered to one source and determining whether they should be sent to another source. The important point is that Web services enable you to create a personalized programmable "valet" that can make decisions for you based upon preferences that you have previously established. And this valet has the potential to reduce the time that you spend managing your computer applications and messaging systems, freeing you up to do more productive tasks.

**Not So Fast...**    There is not much to critique about the foregoing scenario. UDDI's role was minimal, as was that of WSDL. These types of personalized applications are simple—and they can be proven to work today.

The primary concerns are with external infrastructure. (For instance, how do you secure message transfer if you designate messages be sent to a wireless device, or how do you efficiently send a complex multimedia message in such a scenario?) To make Web services ubiquitous, issues such as security, wireless data transfer, multimedia presentation, routing, and numerous details of infrastructure-related technology will need to be resolved. The good news is that the W3C standards organization is already aggressively working on resolving all of these and more.

## Chapter Summary

This chapter focused on how Web services can be used in a variety of business and personal settings to provide efficiencies, to reduce costs, and to deliver other benefits to businesses and individuals. What may be the most important message in this chapter was stated very briefly:

> Web services have the potential to create whole new business models based on services—and thereby change the fundamental basis on which many businesses are run!

This statement should not be taken lightly. As illustrated in the generic examples in this chapter, Web services enable businesses to do the following:

- Rapidly open new markets by making use of external Web services to rapidly assemble application portfolios in order to enter new markets.
- Reduce development costs by making better use of object code that resided internal or external to the organization.
- Streamline operations using Web services combined with business process management software that some vendors now make part-and-parcel of their Web services platform offerings. This streamlining had the result of reducing a business's sales/general/administrative (SG&A) costs—thereby adding greatly to bottom-line profitability.
- Overcome competitive pressure (or create it against competitors) by using Web services protocols and directories to automatically find potential business partners, negotiate services and prices, integrate the service offering into the originator's portfolio—and thus quickly expand an enterprise's application offerings.

- Create new revenue streams by rebuilding existing applications into Web services. By offering nonstrategic applications to the general computer marketplace as services, a company may be able to increase its revenue stream with very little additional programming or administrative effort. And the resulting revenue stream amounts to "found money"—revenue that has been garnered by doing little more than finding a new way to make use of existing intellectual capital.

- Better serve or penetrate existing markets by overcoming obstacles related to traditional product packaging. The Web services model has real potential to upset the traditional packaged-software sales approach used by most independent software vendors. Web services offers potential buyers new options, such as purchasing software as a subscription service hosted by a third-party or by the software vendor itself. Using this model, ISVs that previously had trouble getting users to buy their products because "the IS department is not willing to install and support a given software package" suddenly have a new option—sell directly to the end-users and offer their products as hosted-elsewhere services.

- Overcome system/network interoperability issues. By using Web services, developers can focus more on making applications work together, regardless of underlying infrastructure or platform/language issues. In most cases, users will be completely unaware that services are being provided by cooperating disparate back-end systems—all they will see is the data that they requested being delivered to them in a transparent fashion.

Web services enable businesses to move from a scenario where all applications have to be controlled in-house to a more flexible one where best-of-breed applications can be easily incorporated into the businesses primary application portfolio—creating opportunities for the business to run more efficiently and to adjust to changing competitive and market conditions more nimbly. In other words, by changing the way that applications are designed and developed, business will be made more flexible and efficient. And, as exemplified above, Web services have the potential to alter the fundamental competitive basis for businesses.

The other aspect of Web services described in this chapter has to do with their use to improve personal productivity. In the examples presented, heavy use was made of the messaging services elements of Web services architecture. But messaging is only one of dozens of ways in which Web services will be used to help improve individual productivity in the future. You need to think of personalized Web services as a virtual assistant program. People will be able to automate various elements of their personal lives by having a virtual assistant program find specific informational and data services on the Web and providing the requested information on a specified device within specified timeframes.

Literally tens of thousands of applications are candidates for becoming Web services. Once business realizes the strategic, competitive, or efficiency value of using a Web services approach in application design and deployment, these applications and tens of thousands more will ultimately become Web services enabled.

# 6

# Who Is Using Web Services?

In This
Chapter:

- Anecdotes—examples of *real-world* Web services!

Key Insights:

- Most early adopters are using SOAP protocol to pass XML data between cooperating applications.
- Few early adopters are using UDDI (either to create private registries or to publish applications in public registries).

Giving generic examples, the previous chapter illustrated how Web services could be used to help businesses cut development costs, reduce time-to-market, create/overcome competitive pressure, use repackaging methods to better reach and serve new customers, and create new revenue streams from existing intellectual property. The idea of using Web services to create a personal (but programmatic) valet service for individuals was also introduced. Additionally, in each case, one or more shortcomings of Web services architecture were highlighted—just to make sure that readers understood the difference between what is possible and what is practical with the current state of the art.

This chapter mirrors the previous chapter in terms of organization, but with one big exception: this chapter uses real-world examples to show how Web services are being designed and deployed. Included are examples that illustrate how enterprises are using Web services to create new revenue opportunities, or to reduce development time and costs, or for several other purposes. An example of Microsoft's .NET My Services offerings illustrates how Web services can deliver personalized services in the real world.

Note that .NET My Services is currently being re-evaluated by Microsoft, but the existing services are good examples of personalized services.

The previous chapter covered nine examples of how Web services could be used to affect business strategy as well as how they could be used on a personalized basis. This chapter uses only seven of the nine examples. Examples of how enterprises are using Web services to rapidly expand their applications portfolios and examples of how enterprises are using Web services to create/overcome competitive pressure were not found in the course of this author's research. The likely explanation is that, at this juncture, most Web services solutions are "point product" singular solutions—not far-reaching redevelopment and redeployment of large enterprise application portfolios on a wide scale. (In other words, early adopters are still familiarizing themselves with Web services; they have not yet moved to a broad-based rearchitecting of their portfolios.)

Still, in this chapter you will find that many innovative early adopters are creating new growth opportunities for their enterprises and creating new business models using Web services.

(*Note:* Pay particular attention to how Web services can be used to create a new business model.)

# How Web Services Can Help a Business Open New Markets

Our lead example in this chapter is the open-a-new-market approach being developed by InterPro Global Partners. InterPro views itself as an IT consulting firm that specializes in providing advice to its clients on how to globalize products (translations, packaging, cultural modifications); how to perform application integration; and how to develop Web-based applications. The company has about 160 consultants located in the United States and Europe—and has revenues of over $20 million annually. InterPro has its own application development framework and methodology that helps the company to understand business process flow (how work flows within organizations) and to develop corresponding technical solutions to improve flow efficiency.

Recent advances in Web technologies—specifically the maturation of certain Web standards—now enable InterPro to create applications that perform "Web services" for ad hoc communities of users in healthcare, insurance, financial services, real estate, and dozens of other industries. The company's self-image may be changing from that of an IT consulting firm to that of "a creator and builder of global communities."

SIDEBAR 6-1

INTERPRO (AND BUSINESS PARTNERS) IN THE HEALTHCARE FIELD: OPENING NEW MARKETS

In partnership with Portarius Inc. and IBM, InterPro is developing a Web services-based healthcare community. The physician is at the center of the supply-chain model. Physicians, as members of local Independent Physicians Associations (IPAs), represent the core of local healthcare communities and are at the basis of almost every healthcare transaction. Each healthcare community is comprised of service providers that offer general and highly specialized healthcare services and products. These providers often work in loose association with each other. They have different billing systems, different mail and other collaborative systems, different policies and procedures, and in most cases have patient records that are in paper format—all of which must be streamlined and automated in order to improve overall healthcare efficiency.

InterPro, Portarius, and IBM recognize that inefficiencies exist in the current model. They are working together to aggregate the infrastructure, services, and business model so that healthcare business partners can quickly streamline their interactions with each other and their patients. Portarius brings together the industry expertise and relationships; InterPro is providing the technical and software solutions; and IBM is providing the core infrastructure and national services organization, necessary to deliver on a new vision of healthcare—that of true healthcare process integration. The resulting solution will make it possible for healthcare providers to more easily establish effective and efficient interenterprise business relationships while streamlining business process interactions for all of the participants, lowering transaction costs, and creating new sources of revenue.

## THE USE OF WEB SERVICES STANDARDS

InterPro is making use of all three Web services standards to build its "global communities":

Core to the success of InterPro's global communities is the use of UDDI directories. The company enlists "subscribers" in private directories that are hosted by IBM (IBM has its own UDDI registry). This subscriber approach funds the success of each community that InterPro builds—enticing doctors to use the systems and providing subscribers with additional sales opportunities for their products and services. Using UDDI has enabled InterPro to build a new business model.

WSDL is key to enabling applications to work cooperatively together, InterPro recognizes that mastering WSDL is very important as it seeks to build new Web communities, and the company has invested in training its staff as well as its customers in the design and development of WSDL descriptions according to the standard.

When queried about the use of the SOAP standard, InterPro indicated that the company was integrating SOAP within its own InterProcess Application Development Framework along with other important standards and protocols such as JSP, ASP, EJB, and COM/DCOM technologies (these are programming languages and conventions).

The beauty (from a business perspective) of what InterPro has done for the healthcare community is that its model is replicable. InterPro understands how business processes work, how the Web service technologies work, and how to go about building ad hoc Web communities. Because Inter-Pro and its partners have been able to identify a willing community of doctors who desire access to streamlined interactions with their business partners, and because the company understands business processes and the new Web services technologies, InterPro has been able to develop an approach that attracts laboratories and pharmacies as subscribers who underwrite the cost of running the ad hoc healthcare Web community. In essence, InterPro has birthed a new business model—and this model is fully replicable to other professional communities.

By using its core skills in process flow, technology deployment, and application integration, the company believes that it is ideally positioned for success across these multiple markets.

**Not So Fast...**   This InterPro example illustrates how a company can create new services and bring those services to market using Web services technologies.

As pointed out in previous chapters, strict adherence to Web services standards is not required in order to build Web services applications. InterPro makes use of some Web services standards such as a private UDDI directory to help its business partners find out about each other, and the company uses SOAP to bind sessions. But notice how the company uses Microsoft's COM/DCOM APIs for program-to-program communications instead of WSDL (the reason could be the comparative immaturity of WSDL at this juncture or the fact that the company already had COM/DCOM code available, and using it was the quicker path to market). At most early-adopter sites this kind of mix-and-match approach to building Web services is common, but over time, as Web services directories and other protocols mature, expect Web services standards to dominate as the preferred method of building Web services enabled applications.

Note also how the company has focused on streamlining not only the communications among various business partners but on streamlining the business process itself. This streamlined workflow is where the biggest payback is delivered by this Web service—customers ultimately buy into InterPro's service because it enables them to run their businesses more efficiently.

## How Web Services Can Be Used to Reduce Development Time and Costs

A provider of custom software and consulting services, mhe.net, creates software modules for the financial and technical training industries that can be integrated with third-party solutions to create more robust product offerings.

One such module is mhe.net's SecureCreditServer module—the company's first XML Web service application. This application is used to help industrial product leasing companies accelerate credit verification and thus speed up the credit application approval cycle. (Note how it is used to provide better customer service as well as to improve process efficiency by enabling the rapid processing of applications.)

Not only is this SecureCreditServer module able to help mhe.net customers increase efficiency, it also helps fill in one of the "gotchas" identified earlier in this book by augmenting the security of XML-based transactions (mhe.net's software uses its own security encryption library to help make transactions secure; also it can take advantage of Microsoft's .NET extensive cryptographic library to further extend security features of its product).

SIDEBAR 6-2

USING FEWER AND LESS-SKILLED PROGRAMMERS TO REDUCE COSTS AND TIME-TO-MARKET

Although mhe.net's Secure Credit product helps improve customer service and increase organizational efficiency by streamlining the credit checking process—as well as helps fill in the security gap that exists today in Web services architecture—the effect that Web services (in the form of Microsoft's .NET framework) is having on mhe.net's application development capability is even more impressive. According to Michael Hoenig, President of mhe.net: "We have a unique perspective in this area [the building of Web services applications] since we released our first Web service in Q2, 2000 and have the scars to prove how difficult it is to build a Web service pre-.NET . . . the act of exposing a Visual Basic .NET function as a SOAP compliant Web service is [now] trivial."

When asked how this new ease of development affected mhe.net's application development costs, Mr. Hoenig responded: "I use fewer developers to build an application and they don't have to be rocket scientists, either. When you get to a point of relying on the libraries [application modules], development is more of a mechanical process. Sure, everyone wants something different and you can't build cookie cutters 100% of the time, but if you can box in 90% of the build to implementations of existing code, clients are going to love you."
*Source:* .NET Press Kit from PDC Conference, Microsoft Corporation. Used by Permission.

In this example, mhe.net shows that applications are no longer complex to develop (using the combination of Web services and Microsoft's .NET framework). The company also implies that it no longer needs as many developers with experience in building the infrastructure and plumbing to make distributed applications work. Instead, developers are now used to link libraries of applications modules together to meet client needs rather than dealing with the communications and networking and program-to-program API complexities inherent in pre-Web-services days. By bypassing these complexities, mhe.net can reduce development time and cost. And using less expensive library-linking developers rather than more costly infrastructure-experienced developers also helps reduce development costs and helps the company focus on what it does best: building modules and customizing them to meet specialized customer requirements.

Not So Fast...    In the pre-.NET days, mhe.net had developed SecureCredit-Server using XML-RPC as the transport over HTTP. The latest version built on .NET uses SOAP protocols to bind communications sessions, WSDL protocols, and XML to pass information—all over HTTP. In the case of SecureCreditServer, UDDI is not being used to make the general public aware of mhe.net's security services application, because far-reaching UDDI repositories are not yet in place or in widespread use.

# Another Use of Web Services to Reduce Development Time and Costs

Another firm that used Web services to reduce development costs and ensure the timely delivery of software is the Allegis Corporation. Two important notes about this study: (1) it actually quantifies the amount of time saved using a Web services approach (your mileage may vary); and (2) it was done by a third-party—Gartner Measurement (a division of Gartner Group)—and hence is impartial.

SIDEBAR 6-3
## ALLEGIS CORPORATION—EXECUTIVE SUMMARY

Superior cost-performance along with a powerful development environment and robust toolset were key requirements for Allegis Corporation as they chose to develop their Partner Relationship Management (PRM) applications on a 100% Microsoft and Intel® Architecture-based platform that included Microsoft Windows 2000 Server, Windows 2000 Advanced Server, and the .NET platform running on Intel® two-way PIII and four-way PIII Xeon processors.

**Projected Business and IT Benefit**

- Faster time-to-market Up 28%
- Customer solutions development time Down 28%
- New customers from improved integration Up 20%
- Configuration of customer solutions Up 27%
- Maintain SLAs of 99.5% uptime 100%

The REJ business value analysis validated Allegis' assertion that the .NET platform operating on Microsoft Windows 2000 Server and Advanced Server is the most efficient use of corporate financial and human resources. This solution provides a 28% faster development cycle to get the Allegis eBusiness Suite to market and 27% faster configuration of customer solutions than that achieved in a UNIX-based environment. Using .NET technologies, Allegis is able to increase revenue growth by responding more quickly to changing market conditions and to the ever-increasing demands of their rapidly expanding PRM customer base. One immediate result of a quicker development cycle is that Allegis can implement two product updates a year—a very rapid development cycle for enterprise software—for its Global 2000 customers. The scalability and reliability of Windows 2000 Server directly support Allegis' ability to quickly develop new application modules, guarantee 99.5%

uptime in their Service Level Agreements (SLAs), and build seamless interoperability and integration with legacy databases and IT systems, thereby closing an anticipated 20% more business.

"Choosing Microsoft's .NET platform was a key strategic decision for Allegis," said David Story, Vice President of Engineering at Allegis Corporation. "Allegis took advantage of the .NET platform to pioneer the delivery of enterprise-level PRM solutions in both installed and hosted options. Using .NET Enterprise Servers in [calendar year] 2000, we delivered 99.97% software availability for our hosted Global 2000 customers, and we developed the software faster than on a UNIX-based alternative. Our use of open standards, such as Extensible Markup Language (XML) and Simple Open Access Protocol (SOAP), promotes easy integration with other companies and programs, improves our enterprise software design and ultimately is a reason why we lead our market."

"Our choice of the .NET platform has allowed us to achieve impressive results in less than two years due to rapid development and deployment cycles and lower operational costs," noted Greg Price, Director of Business Development for Allegis. "Getting to market faster presents greater opportunities for increasing revenue." The REJ business value analysis, assessed by Gartner Measurement, a business unit of the GartnerGroup, confirmed that using the .NET platform and Microsoft SQL Server™ 7.0 and Internet Information Server running on Intel Architecture-based Windows 2000 Advanced Servers enables Allegis to simultaneously maintain 99.97% uptime, a low-cost hardware infrastructure and very low overhead hosting expenses. Allegis implemented a 100% Windows and Intel development and hosted application infrastructure at their inception in 1998, deployed it in 1999 and used Windows 2000 Server and the .NET platform since the summer of 2000.

*Source:* http://www.microsoft.com/BUSINESS/casestudies/microsoft_allegis.asp. Used by Permission.

## How Web Services Can Be Used to Help Create New Organizational Efficiencies

Storebrand (pronounced "Story-brand") is Norway's largest financial and insurance company—a diversified financial services provider that provides health and life insurance as well as banking and asset management services to more than 280,000 clients throughout Norway.

In this highly competitive market Storebrand is well positioned for continued growth. For instance, by using innovative techniques and packaging, Storebrand Life (the company's life insurance unit) allows customers to "link" products together (such as defined contribution occupational pension products with individual investment choices) to determine how aggressively their pension funds are invested. Linking other products and services together—and finding new distributors for these products—is expected to be key to the company's continued growth.

Also important to continued growth will be the company's ability to control costs by introducing internal efficiencies as well as efficiencies in dealing with its business partners. The company knows that if it can automate certain business processes, it can lower operating costs, and those cost savings pass directly to the company's bottom line.

Sidebar 6-4
## Storebrand: Using Business Process Management and Web Services to Reduce Operating Costs

Imagine serving 6,500 companies with approximately 390,000 employees—and having to synchronize the records of those employees such that individual coverage could be accurately calculated for each employee under a variety of insurance schemes. For Storebrand, this monumental synchronization task has largely been a manual process that involves the verification, updating, and rechecking of data before it is entered into Storebrand's centralized database. And this process has been begging for an automated solution—a solution that heretofore has not been forthcoming using existing Web standards.

Storebrand has attacked this problem in two ways: (1) by modifying its existing manual practices (in other words, changing its internal business processes such that people do not have to get as heavily involved in handling pension calculation and input into Storebrand's mainframe database); and (2) by enabling employee data to be captured from client payroll systems using electronic Web services, automatically performing calculations on that data, and then directly transferring the resulting information directly to its mainframe database.

As a result of automating this manual process, Storebrand has been able to improve operational efficiency by reassigning a number of employees who are currently involved in the manual pension calculation/input task to other tasks (thereby making better use of people and potentially saving money by not having to hire new employees to do other manual tasks). Storebrand's automation of this pension calculation/input task is expected to save the company thousands of hours in manual labor costs annually.

To assist in this effort Storebrand employed the assistance of IBM's jStart team (www.ibm.com/software/jstart) to help with the implementation of Web services. The project team identified the following objectives:

- Create Web services for Storebrand (as Servlets);
- Adapt vendor payroll systems to do Web services;
- Implement necessary infrastructure;
- Connect existing Storebrand business partners; and
- Provide a proof-of-concept to Storebrand that Web services can reduce operating costs.

Storebrand, with IBM's assistance, accomplished these goals. The product design involved the following:

To get the divergent environments [Windows-based and mainframe databases, as well as customer/business partner environments] to share data, jStart suggested using a SOAP (Simple Object Access Protocol) connection to bridge the gap by connecting the Windows environments of most payroll applications with the WebSphere Java environment at Storebrand Life.

The team determined that three options were available:

SOAP alone—SOAP would provide the basic program-to-program "glue" that enables applications to bind together and enter into peer-to-peer communications.

SOAP + WSDL definitions—WSDL would provide a standardized description of the service, but would not offer full repository lookup. Once the application service has been described, it would be published with a service broker that helps make the application/service known to Web "requestors" (in this case, new Storebrand distributors).

SOAP + WSDL + UDDI (including service description in registry)—UDDI is also a framework for Web services integration. It contains standards-based specifications to describe the Storebrand products and services and allow discovery in a global registry architecture.

Storebrand initially opted to utilize a combination of all three technologies. To do this, the team created a COM object that takes the XML document as input and sends it to the Storebrand Web service, by transmitting it over the Internet via the HTTP protocol. The customer sites, in this case, primarily used Microsoft Windows NT or 2000 systems to perform their data entry for the benefits processing. Thus, the team decided on building COM interfaces in VB for the client-side and used Microsoft's SOAP toolkit for the interface. On Storebrand's server-side, the team converted an existing Java application to a service by simply using the Wizard provided in the IBM XML & Web Services Development Environment. This Web services enabled application receives the XML document and transforms the data for the verification and update process required to feed the DB2 central database of Storebrand. Data transport and manipulation at the backend is managed with MQSeries Integrator. *Source:* http://www-106.ibm.com/developerworks/library/ws-asa/. Used by Permission.

Notice that Storebrand was able to use all of the most important Web services protocols in unison to create a sweeping, cross-platform program-to-program solution that enabled the company to reduce human overhead costs. Also notice how IBM's WebSphere platform made it possible to augment Web services protocols with other protocols and messaging services (such as its MQSeries Integrator) in order to enable cross-platform interoperability. Of all of the examples in this book, Storebrand made the most comprehensive use of Web services in creating its solution.

By making use of XML to capture and present data, by modifying business processes between Storebrand and its customers, and by using the SOAP Web standard for program-to-program communications, *the company will now be able to save thousands of hours in information capture and input time—thus reducing costs related to manual information processing.*

## Storebrand's Web Services Plans Beyond Creating Organizational Efficiency

In its first pilot project Storebrand learned how to exploit Web services technologies to improve organizational efficiency and lower operating costs. The company is now looking at how to make use of these technologies in other business areas within its Storebrand Bank and Storebrand Funds business units in order to increase operating efficiency.

One plan involves finding new distributors and opening up new sources of income. Storebrand plans to exploit UDDI, WSDL, and SOAP to open new business-to-business opportunities for the company. The company sees three potential benefits of using Web services for application design and business-partner integration:

- Being able to make its services known to the industry (using UDDI).

- Being able to publish details about how to work with Storebrand applications (using WSDL).
- Being able to communicate easily with distributors and clients who are using different systems architectures (using SOAP)—in order to provide the company with new revenue growth opportunities by enticing new and existing distributors to resell Storebrand products.

**Not So Fast...** Observe that many of Storebrand's customers operate their payroll systems on the Windows 2000 operating environment on Intel-based systems architectures. Meanwhile, Storebrand's central data repository operates on an IBM mainframe running a completely different operating environment. To get the two environments to share data, Storebrand and its customers developed a means for the Windows 2000 payroll environments to convert data to an XML-based data stream that is then sent to Storebrand's mainframe using SOAP as a means to communicate between two diverse systems environments. The sharing of information between Storebrand and its customers was based on using Microsoft COM protocols, not WSDL (although WSDL was used to describe the Web service being provided between Windows and enterprise server environments). Over time Storebrand will probably migrate to more extensive use of WSDL protocols for this application, but for the sake of expediency COM protocols were used as a short-term solution.

# How Web Services Can Help Create a New Revenue Stream from Existing Intellectual Property

Sabre is the worldwide leader in providing information technology solutions for the travel and transportation industry. The company is best known for its innovative travel and reservation systems, used by travel agents and corporate travel departments for almost thirty years as a means to handle flight reservations and hotel room bookings and to provide numerous other travel-related services. But the company is also known within the industry for providing travel-related consulting and software development and for the outsourcing reservation systems for its customer base.

As a leading-edge exploiter of technology, Sabre constantly looks for new technologies that it can use to help broaden its customer base or service its customers better. As part of its strategic due diligence, the company has closely watched the evolution of UDDI, WSDL, and SOAP—and believes that these standards can be highly instrumental in helping the company open new sources of revenue while helping its customers improve operational efficiency.

In this example Sabre makes use of an existing software program—the "Hotel Shopper"—to expand into new low-end markets using Web services. In so doing, Sabre is able to increase its revenue stream by taking existing intellectual material and reaugmenting it to serve new customers.

SIDEBAR 6-5
## SABRE INCORPORATED—USING EXISTING INTELLECTUAL PROPERTY TO CREATE A NEW REVENUE STREAM

Travel agencies spend thousands to hundreds of thousands of dollars annually using people-time to manually make phone calls or visit Web sites to look up hotel availability, accommodations, and costs. In its application portfolio Sabre has a hotel location/booking application (called the "Hotel Shopper"). This application enables Sabre's business partners to search for hotel rooms by geography (for instance, helping to find all the hotels in the area of Hollywood and Vine streets or near the Eiffel Tower). It also automatically indicates if the hotels being evaluated have available space and helps determine the type of accommodations and prices for rooms. Many of Sabre's larger customers have highly skilled programmers who have been able to write specialized programs that interface with Sabre's Passenger Services System to gain access to the Hotel Shopper program. (These specialized programs access Sabre's system using complex "command-level" programs.) A description of the ins-and-outs of writing "command-level" interfaces is not important—what matters is that writing such interfaces between a client system and a Sabre system requires sophisticated and costly skills (generally not in the range of technical competence or cost for most small businesses and even some mid-sized businesses). The use of Web services protocols provides a means for Sabre's small- and mid-sized business partners to easily interface with Sabre's Hotel Shopper application. Instead of having to write complex command-level interfaces to access Sabre's Passenger Services System that houses its Hotel Shopper application, Sabre's small- and mid-sized business partners can use much simpler WSDL and SOAP protocols to get access to Hotel Shopper.

This example illustrates how Sabre was able to leverage an existing application (the Hotel Shopper) to better serve its existing customers as well as open new opportunities to market its services to new customers. By making it extremely easy for all kinds of small-, medium-, and large sized business customers to interface with its Hotel Shopper system, the company has opened-up new revenue opportunities for itself using existing intellectual material.

Now, take this situation and extrapolate a bit. Suppose Sabre were to decide that the Hotel Shopper application was not a "strategic" application. (At present, this is not the case, but we're just supposing.) Should Sabre make this application available industrywide as a Web service, the company could open up a new source of revenue by charging a fee (a micropayment) every time any travel agency made use of it. If this application were to be heavily used by travel agents industrywide, Sabre could make a lot of money (thus creating a new revenue source for the company). Further, if the company were to make dozens of other applications available as Web services, the company could stand to make even more money. In this "pretend" example, notice how Sabre's business model would be shifted by the use of a Web services approach to offering its products to market on an open/micropayment basis to the mass travel agency marketplace.

Not So Fast...   By making use of Web service protocols Sabre has been able to extend an already existing application (the Hotel Shopper) to its existing business partners and to prospective new customers. To do this Sabre has used simple-to-implement WSDL and SOAP Web services protocols. Note, though, that the company has not yet listed these services in a public UDDI registry—hence the location of this newly Web-enabled service is not generally known to the travel industry.

At the time of this writing it was unclear what Sabre's ultimate plans were for using UDDI directories. The company could create a private UDDI directory service for its clients such that they could gain access to a suite of Web-enabled applications. Or the company could ultimately make all or part of its application portfolio available to the travel agency market in the form of Web services. Or the company could choose to do neither.

# How Web Services Can Help ISVs Repackage Their Software Offerings to Better Reach/Serve Existing Markets

Web services present independent software vendors (ISVs) with several new options to repackage applications as "hosted services" that can be sold on a per-seat, per-use, or subscription basis to existing clients and new prospects.

Here is an example of such repackaging:

SIDEBAR 6-6

## VISUALIZE, INC.—USING WEB SERVICES TO REPACKAGE EXISTING APPLICATIONS TO OPEN NEW MARKETS

Visualize, Inc. is a maker of data-visualization software—the kind of software that enables decision makers to view "flat" two-dimensional (height and width) data in three dimensions (height, width, and depth). This kind of software is highly useful in helping business decision makers take spreadsheet-type data and visualize it using three-dimensional charts.

Recently, a number of Visualize prospects have expressed a desire to use Visualize software, but they have been unable to persuade their IT departments to install, run, and manage Visualize code. These prospects have shown a preference for having data-visualization software hosted by some other company and provided to them as a service.

By making some of its data-visualization products available as a "Web service," Visualize can offer its data-visualization software as a chargeable service. By listing its product in a UDDI directory (a planned activity), the company will be able to make itself "known" to other applications. By offering its product as a service, the company may be able to actually charge more because it provides an application and a processing service for its customers.

This Visualize example is interesting from multiple perspectives. As a small company, Visualize needs to find ways to broaden its market share as well as ways to contain costs. By repackaging some of its software products, Visualize is hoping to make it easier for some potential buyers to use them (because those prospective buyers would not need their IT department to install and maintain the software). Making the software easier to buy should help increase market share.

From a cost-of-doing-business perspective, when Visualize ultimately lists its products in public UDDI directories, the company should be able to reduce its cost of doing business by lowering its SG&A costs. Here's how this scenario could work:

Right now Visualize markets its products using a direct sales force and business partners. But, as some of its products are listed in UDDI directories, applications will seek out Visualize services and some day negotiate how to pay for those services. When this happens, Visualize will not have to use a direct sales force for missionary sales—instead, applications will find Visualize products and determine whether and how they can use them. Fewer direct sales representatives would be required to "push" Visualize products to market.

## How Web Services Can Help Solve Legacy Systems Incompatibility Problems

This scenario resembles the previous Sabre scenario in that Dollar Rent A Car Systems is using Web services to make a reservation system available to its business partners and customers. This example is used in this section because Dollar Rent A Car uses Web services on the back end (between UNIX- and Windows-based systems) for data-transfer interoperability purposes.

SIDEBAR 6-7

DOLLAR RENT A CAR: USING WEB SERVICES FOR SYSTEMS INTEROPERABILITY

Headquartered in Tulsa, Oklahoma, Dollar Rent A Car Systems Inc. is one of the world's largest rental car agencies. The company has 430 worldwide offices located in 26 countries and has almost 100,000 vehicles in inventory in the United States. In the first quarter of 2000 one of Dollar's business partners, Southwest Airlines, offered Dollar the opportunity to put a link to the Dollar rental car reservations system

on Southwest's Web site such that customers could make plane and car reservations at the same time. But to do this required Dollar to be able to link its Windows-based reservation system with Southwest's UNIX/CORBA-based systems.
Instead of building a fixed-address CORBA-compliant application (which is how Dollar might have had to interface with Southwest in pre-Web services days), Dollar chose to make use of XML as the data default format and SOAP protocols for binding the UNIX- and Windows-based databases together. By taking this approach Dollar was able to build a flexible solution that it could potentially offer to other airlines—as well as being able to avoid a long-term code maintenance commitment (to maintain CORBA code). Using this approach, Dollar was able to architect a data translation system between its database and Southwest's differing database.
*Source:* http://www.microsoft.com/BUSINESS/casestudies/b2c/dollarrentacar.asp. Used by Permission.

What is particularly interesting about this scenario is that Dollar used Web services products to build a bridge between two disparate system types and databases. In other words, Dollar used Web services to foster systems interoperability between back-end UNIX- and Windows-based systems. From a customer/user's perspective this database translation is transparent—the user is completely unaware that any data translation is taking place between the Southwest and Dollar systems platforms.

**Not So Fast...**     What is not immediately apparent in this scenario is that Southwest remained faithful to its CORBA-based approach to handling distributed applications. What Dollar did was build a Web services-based system that could take CORBA requests and translate them into SOAP requests for data on Dollar systems. Going the other way, the Dollar Web services system translated the SOAP data back into an envelope that Southwest's CORBA system could handle (and sent that data to a specified port). In this case Web services was used to foster system-to-system interoperability, but notice that the translations to and from the CORBA system all took place at Dollar (because Southwest does not use Web services protocols for this application at this time).

# How Web Services Improve Individual Productivity

The preceding chapter talked about "personalizable" Web services, consisting essentially of programs that can act on a user's behalf to carry out the user's bidding. An outstanding example of such a program can be found in Microsoft's .NET My Services family of products—more specifically in the company's .NET Alerts implementation.

.NET My Services is a product category that houses (and will house) programs that can act on a user's behalf that also make use of Web services protocols and registries. .NET Alerts is one such program in the .NET My Services collection of programs. .NET Alerts is a program that computer users can use to receive requested alerts from authorized information providers. For instance, .NET Alerts can be used to send information to you from stock service at a particular time of day or even when a particular stock threshold has been met. When this information is received at the user's chosen e-mail address (in the form of a simple XML message), it can then be forwarded from the e-mail inbox to a desktop, handheld, PDA, or any Internet-ready device that the user chooses to assign. A program that acts on behalf of the user determines where the user is, whether the user has authorized this particular type of information to be sent, and then sends an e-mail notification that directs the user where to go to get the information he or she has requested.

Because .NET Alerts can act on someone's behalf to carry out a sorting task that a person normally would have to do manually, .NET Alerts increase individual productivity. Notice that they also offer businesses an effective way to reach their customers and provide them with options to take particular "actions." Additionally, notice that .NET Alerts can stop businesses from spamming (sending unwanted information and e-mails) to consumers (because consumers can instruct their personal .NET Alert applications to send only the mail and messages that they request).

Microsoft's Web site indicates that .NET Alerts can be used for much more than just sending e-mail or Web-based content. For example, a business could alert its customers when:

- An item is back in stock. (Click to buy the item.)
- An item on their wish list went on sale. (Click to buy the item.)
- They were outbid at an auction. (Click to raise your bid.)
- An important news story just broke. (Click to read.)
- Their order has shipped. (Click to track.)

*Source*: http://Microsoft.com/MYSERVICES/alerts/default.asp. Used by Permission.

**Not So Fast...**  As has been the case in almost every previous example, .NET Alerts does not make heavy use of UDDI directories to provide Web services. But .NET Alerts does make heavy use of SOAP protocols to enable messages and information to be sent to multiple different device types. Also note: Microsoft's .NET My Services are currently being re-evaluated by Microsoft.

## Chapter Summary

A walk through today's Web services landscape reveals several very interesting ways to make use of Web services to increase business revenue, foster systems interoperability, reach new customers, and reduce software development costs. It should also be noted, though, that no good examples were found of enterprises that are using Web services to dramatically expand their applications portfolio. Nor were examples found of the use of Web services to create and rapidly counteract competitive pressure. One is left to conclude that Web services applications are still in the experimental, nonmainstream phase of evolution.

Still, a close look at the anecdotes presented in this chapter shows that Web services are now being used to repackage existing ISV applications in order to make them more appealing to prospective buyers. And Web services applications can indeed be used to foster interoperability between dissimilar, disparate systems platforms and databases. Further, Web services can be used to reduce SG&A costs—both by reducing manual processing tasks and by making it possible to sell products without having a direct or indirect sales force aggressively "pushing" solutions to market.

An illustrative example on the personalization front was Microsoft's .NET My Services product suite. Other personalized Web services, too, are being brought to market. For instance, Sun and a number of its business partners recently announced the "Liberty Alliance" in order to provide automated password and credit card services to consumers. (This alliance has been designed to compete with Microsoft's "Passport" functionality.) Most suppliers of application server platforms provide software tools that allow applications to be personalized for use by consumers. In other words, although Microsoft's .NET Alerts were illustrated in this chapter, other vendors are also active in the personalized Web services arena.

Dozens of excellent examples on various Web sites prove that Web services really do work—and that they can be applied in many ways to help organizations and individuals achieve their particular goals. The shortfall is that few public UDDI directories exist—and this prevents many ISVs from effectively marketing their products and services. Overall, however, a walk through the dozens and dozens of Web services Web sites, and talks with Web services users, suggest that Web services may indeed have the "traction" to become the distributed computing standard that many IS managers and business executives have long been waiting for.

# 7

# When Should My Organization Adopt Web Services?

So far in this book we have defined Web services, seen how they work in generic and real-world environments, and discussed the relative strengths and shortcomings of Web services architecture as compared to other approaches such as CORBA or COM. With respect to short-comings, we explored the view that basic Web services registries and protocols are appropriate for low-volume, light-transactional applications at present, unless augmented with ancillary products that enhance security, reliability, quality of service and the like.

But in the previous chapter, we saw numerous examples of successful Web services application deployments, some of them in mission-critical, run-the-business situations.

So, given these conflicting perspectives, how do you decide when your organization should adopt Web services? This chapter examines some of the dynamics that may play a role in your decision-making process.

## The Types of Questions You Need to Ask Yourself

The answer to the "when" question depends on a number of different factors, some of which include:

- How far along in terms of competency is your organization with the development of application objects and components?
- Does your development organization understand store-and-forward messaging architecture?
- Do you have any customized applications that you may wish to sell on the open market?
- Do you have an opportunity to gain competitive advantage using Web services object components?
- Do you have an opportunity to reduce your cost of development for new applications using a Web services developmental approach?

Notice that these questions isolate two elements: (1) the level of object-oriented programming/messaging competency within your organization; and (2) an opportunity to reduce costs or open new markets. If your staff has the programming skills necessary to build Web services—and if you can identify low-transaction, high-payback opportunities that can make use of a message-passing, store-and-forward architecture (which is what a program-to-program architecture like Web services is)—then you can embark today on building Web services applications. On the other hand, if your programming staff does not have the required skills—or if you can't isolate a business opportunity that can exploit Web services—the time is not right for you to start building Web services applications.

## Where Is Most of the Activity Taking Place Today?

One useful way to determine when your organization should engage in building Web services is to look at where other organizations are focusing their initial Web services development efforts. Today, the biggest payback using Web services can be found in (1) improving internal business efficiency and reducing developmental costs; (2) conducting certain business-to-business (B2B) transactions; and (3) providing a slew of new "individual" services (such as anytime, anywhere, to-any-Internet-device messaging for individual users).

Let's take a closer look. First, Web services are being used to develop new customized applications. The InterPro and mhe.net examples in the previous chapters are good examples.

Second, Web services are being used in the automation of certain business-to-business transactions. Web services are far easier to implement than many of today's cumbersome Electronic Data Interchange (EDI) applications (which are used by many businesses to package information and share that information with business partners). And supplier-to-supplier B2B transactions are usually based on message passing (as are Web services). By reducing programming complexity and by taking advantage of the Web services message-passing architectural basis, Web services are growing well in this B2B market segment.

Third, Web services are being used to make available new "automated attendant" programs that can help people manage messaging and automate other elements of their personal or professional lives.

Web services (particularly UDDI and WSDL) are being used internal to the organization to help enterprises create an inventory of application modules (this inventory serves to provide application developers with a useful in-house object code repository that can be used to help them reuse rather than rewrite code). The primary benefit derived from "inventorying" existing applications is that an organization gains an understanding of what modules it has already developed or has at its disposal—and this can help reduce or eliminate redundant programming efforts by developers who are not aware that an application module may already exist within an enterprise.

In other words, if your organization:

- Is currently undertaking the development of new, customized applications, then using a Web services approach may be justified now. Note, however, that you must determine the level of security, transaction rates, and reliability of your new custom application—and supplement Web services with other products and services that can bolster your custom application in those areas. If security, high transaction rates, and reliability are primary concerns, it may or may not be the right time for you to implement Web services (depending on your level of confidence in using third-party products to augment your Web application server);
- Has a large inventory of object-oriented application modules (as many software development and professional services firms do), then your organization may be ripe for adopting UDDI and WSDL protocols today;
- Is looking for a potentially easier way to build B2B transactions, Web services may (or may not) be appropriate (depending on security, transaction, and reliability requirements);
- Is looking to open new market opportunities (such as the InterPro scenario in the previous chapter), then it probably should examine Web services architecture; or
- Is trying to provide personalized automated attendant

services for consumers and customers, then Web services may prove to be an appropriate design architecture for building such applications.

## Pay Close Attention to UDDI

There is a school of thought that believes Web services will really start to take off when public UDDI directories/registries become more widespread. Essentially, once these directories are in place, enterprises will be able to find a wealth of object-oriented applications that can be automatically integrated with enterprise applications to provide enterprises with additional functionality. These Web services applications would be made available for a fee (which is how some of the Web services applications makers would make money), or in some cases for free.

As shown in Figure 7–1, Gartner Group (a highly respected research and analysis firm) estimates that Web services will really start to take off in 2005 as public UDDI directories emerge and mature.

**2001**   Web services tooling delivered. Developers buy new on-site development tools, begin building vital Web services.

**2002**   Business Web services begin to appear in large numbers. Mass-connected B2C Web services already in place.

**2003**   UDDI Registry adoption grows in significance. Private registries proliferate to support private exchanges. Government use of Web accelerates significantly.

**2004**   Business adoption of Web services-based models. Services-centered computing enters adolescence. Private registries still dominate revenue-generation models, and channel opportunities are commonplace. Forty percent of financial services transactions leverage Web services model. Thirty-five percent of government services are delivered as Web services.

**2005**   Public UDDI Registries gain attention as public exchanges. Dynamic services gain more attention.

FIGURE 7-1   When Will Your Organization Need to Adopt Web Services? *Source:* "Web Services: Software as Service Comes Alive," Daryl Plummer, October 2001. Used by Permission.

## Chapter Summary

When should your organization adopt Web services? The answer depends largely on two factors: (1) the skill set of your programmers (particularly in the areas of object programming and messaging architecture), and (2) your organization's need (open new markets, reduce development costs, etc.).

As illustrated in earlier chapters, hundreds of organizations are currently using Web services to perform a variety of tasks. Visit www.Xmethods.com, as well as Microsoft and IBM Web sites, for examples of customers and applications that have currently been developed.

Much activity to date in terms of Web services development has been focused on B2B transactions as well as on reducing application development costs.

From a B2B perspective the important point is that Web services are based on a message-passing store-and-forward architecture that lends itself nicely to conducting transactions between business partners. And writing XML and Web services applications is reported to be easier than using EDI (although EDI is more sophisticated, reliable, and secure at the present time).

With respect to reducing application development costs, many enterprises are starting to consolidate all of their application objects into internal registries. They hope to reduce development costs by encouraging application developers to make use of already existing application objects rather than constantly reinventing-the-wheel with redundant application objects.

Finally, many organizations are starting to recognize that Web services offer them the potential to open new markets, or to service existing markets in new and different ways.

When should your organization adopt Web services? *Now*—if your organization has a need to consolidate existing application objects, or can take advantage of Web services to reduce application development costs, or has found a way to open new markets. *By 2005*—if your organization is looking to capitalize on a vast application database that will manifest itself in public UDDI directories of the future.

# part III

## A Business Executive Buyer's Guide

# 8

# What Vendor Selection Criteria Should Be Used?

f, having gained an understanding of the strategic implications and pitfalls of Web services technologies, you decide that now is the time for your enterprise to start experimenting with and prototyping Web services applications, then you may be asking yourself how to get started. This chapter explains where you can turn to obtain Web services products and services. The next chapter will provide you with a closer look (vendor by vendor) at the leading suppliers of these products and services.

# How Do You Build/Acquire Web Services Applications? Three Approaches

At present there are three basic approaches to building/acquiring Web services based applications:

1. The first involves choosing a business partner (a systems/software supplier) that offers a turnkey *application server* platform tuned and optimized for the creation of Web services applications. Such platforms typically offer other software products that help developers and IS managers to

   • Develop, present, and deploy applications.

   • Manage, secure, and otherwise enhance systems infrastructure.

   • Optimize business process flow, or resolve interoperability issues (such as messaging) with legacy or non-Web-services-enabled systems environments.

   There are two classes of prospective application server business partners from which to choose: (1) those that offer a *completely tuned application development environment, associated hardware, and professional services*; and (2) those that primarily *focus on building robust application development environments and related infrastructure extensions (such as security and management), and that may also provide integrated value-added software*, such as business process management, personalization, and the like). This second class of supplier may or may not actually sell systems hardware or provide related professional services.

2. A second approach involves purchasing or obtaining the individual tools and utilities that can help you build Web services applications a la carte (individually). In using this approach, an enterprise takes on much of the responsibility for integrating various application components. Additionally, should that enterprise want to further enhance its application server environment with business process management software or some other value-added software, it would have to find the appropriate software and potentially provide the integration work needed to integrate it with the source application server. An example of this approach is the use of certain open-source products to assemble your own Web services application development environment. For instance, the open-source Apache XML project provides various tools and utilities that can be used to help build XML Web services applications, as shown in the list below.

SIDEBAR 8-1
## THE XML APACHE PROJECT—TOOLS AND UTILITIES THAT CAN BE USED FOR BUILDING WEB SERVICES

1. Xerces—XML parsers in Java, C++ (with Perl and COM bindings)

2. Xalan—XSLT stylesheet processors, in Java and C++

3. Cocoon—XML-based Web publishing, in Java

4. FOP—XSL formatting objects, in Java

5. Xang—Rapid development of dynamic server pages, in JavaScript

6. SOAP—Simple Object Access Protocol

7. Batik—A Java-based toolkit for Scalable Vector Graphics (SVG)

8. Crimson—A Java XML parser derived from the Sun Project X Parser.

*Source:* http://xml.apache.org/. Used by Permission.

3. A third approach is to work with professional service firms that offer Web services application development expertise.

A potential fourth approach is also expected to evolve over time. This approach will allow an enterprise to "farm-out" its entire IT infrastructure and Web services applications development to application solution providers (ASPs). The ASPs will assemble and run the enterprise's information infrastructure, using Web services to dynamically build the enterprise's application portfolio. In this case the ASP becomes a kind of professional services firm that develops applications as well as an outsourcer for designing, maintaining, and operating an enterprise's IT environment.

At this juncture no ASPs are positioned to offer this kind of comprehensive Web services portfolio development and outsourcing service, owing primarily to the relative immaturity of Web services today. (Web services are just not robust enough to base an entire business on.) Because of this immaturity, the marketplace is not yet ready to build businesses exclusively on a Web services application development model. But it is reasonable to extrapolate that in the future, as Web services mature and can be proven to be enterprise robust and capable of handling complex transactions in a secure fashion, the ASP market will come alive with Web services development and hosting offerings. Over time, ASPs will combine infrastructure and application deployment expertise to help enterprises build, deploy, and manage large portfolios of Web services applications.

## A Closer Look at the Application Server Marketplace

The next thing to understand about Web services is that *there is no Web services marketplace*. Instead, Web services are part of a large, established "integration/application server" marketplace.

What is an integration/application server? It is a turnkey system that includes software for application development, application deployment, and extensions (such as personalization or wireless device integration) that make it possible to easily build and deploy component (object-based) applications. Figure 1–3 shows one such server platform, illustrating the structure of an IBM WebSphere platform. IBM, Sun, Hewlett-Packard, and others all supply J2EE-based application servers. BEA provides Web services software as well as other application tools and utilities that run on various vendor platforms (but the company does not sell hardware). Microsoft sells its own application language environment (C#) plus other languages, tools, utilities, and value-added software that can run on Intel-based platforms (but Microsoft does not sell systems hardware).

Microsoft's strategy is known as .NET, Sun Microsystem's is Sun ONE, HP's is Netaction, and Oracle's is Dynamic services. All are making a run at becoming major players in this marketplace. The stakes are high: revenues in the application server marketplace totaled almost $1.7 billion in 2001 and are expected to top $9 billion in 2003, according to projections by Boston-based Giga Group. A big reason for the fierce competition is that IS buyers, once they have made their decision on a platform, tend to stick with it—so winning big now is expected to help competitors win even bigger deals in the future.

As mentioned previously, Web services involve far more than just the implementation of certain protocols and directory/registry standards. Application servers fill in the gaps with additional presentation, process, and development/ integration elements that are needed in order to expeditiously build Web services applications.

The primary benefit of using an all-inclusive application server approach to building Web services applications is that your supplier has done a lot of the integration and optimization work for you—so that your developers do not need to spend a lot of time trying to get various application tools and utilities to work together. For instance, most of these application servers include tools that allow application developers to create applications, then automatically compile those applications and automatically optimize the business process flow of those applications. These integrated product suites save a lot of time and eliminate a lot of application development complexity for developers, resulting in decreased product development cycles and less application development cost for enterprises that use application server products and tools.

## First-Pass Look at the Market Positioning of Some of the Application Server Competitors

Each of these vendors will be examined in considerably more detail in Chapter 10 but at this juncture it is important to briefly illustrate how these products have been optimized.

In the case of IBM, the company offers its WebSphere suite of application development tools and utilities as well as other value-added software on multiple operating environments (Linux, OS/400, Windows, and others), and WebSphere can be run on PowerPC- or Intel-based systems. In the case of Sun, Sun ONE can be run on Sun's UNIX (Solaris) on Sun's UltraSparc microprocessor architecture. And with HP, NetAction has been designed to serve both HP/UX and Windows environments.

Notice each of these vendor's strategies. Each sells an integrated suite of application development environment tools and utilities that ultimately serve to drive the sale of that vendor's hardware platform(s). And all of these vendors have professional services organizations, so each also has an opportunity to garner service revenue by selling turnkey application server environments. In short: selling an application development environment leads directly to the sale of related hardware and to the potential sale of professional services.

Contrast this approach with the approach taken by BEA and Microsoft—vendors that sell application server environments but do not focus on selling hardware. BEA's WebLogic can run across multiple systems platforms, but BEA does not seek to garner hardware revenue. Likewise, Microsoft's .NET products can be sold on various vendors' Intel-based servers, but Microsoft does not concentrate on making revenue from the sale of systems hardware (they leave that to their partners like Compaq, Dell, HP, and others). Notice that the strategy for these application server environment creators has to do with selling licenses, not proliferating hardware sales.

In the case of BEA the company makes substantial revenue by providing professional services related to applications design and deployment using BEA products. Microsoft, on the other hand, has a several thousand professional services personnel but focuses on specialty application development using advanced Microsoft technologies. This company makes a concerted effort to let its business partners garner professional services revenue. So, for some software makers professional services may be a strategically important revenue stream, while others leave professional services revenue for their business partners.

Each strategy can be used successfully, but it is important for you to understand your potential business partner's motivations before committing to a long-term application server and development environment relationship.

## Chapter Summary

There are three general approaches to obtaining Web services products and services. First, you can purchase a turnkey, all-inclusive application server that includes application development environment tools and utilities as well as other value-added software (such as personalization or business process management software). Second, you can use a do-it-yourself approach using either point (a la carte) software products or open-source products that you and your organization take responsibility for integrating. And third, you can employ a professional services firm (and let them choose the approach for architecting Web services environments for you).

In practice, however, most of the early, real-world competition in the Web services space is coming from the providers of turnkey application server environments. These Web services platform providers are:

1. Vendors that build and sell completely integrated systems software, application development environments, hardware, and services.

**2.** Vendors that build application development environments that can be sold on multiple different systems platforms [these are generally vendors that in the past built Enterprise Application Integration (EAI) environments].

Vendors that include hardware, software, and services include IBM (with WebSphere); Sun (with Sun ONE); and HP with NetAction. Vendors that build application development environments include BEA and Microsoft (these vendors focus on software sales—not necessarily on professional services revenues—and not at all on hardware revenue.

Other approaches to building Web services environments include building your own using point products, and finding a professional services firm that excels in Web services development and deployment. The build-your-own approach involves finding and integrating the tools and utilities needed to build Web services applications, but it costs considerably less than buying a completely integrated application development suite from application server vendors. The primary benefits are the following:

- Using open-source software can be considerably less expensive than purchasing a complete soup-to-nuts application server.
- Using point products (single software products that are designed to address a particular need versus the previously described application server approach that requires that customers purchase several products—sometimes a whole development suite of products) can be more efficient.
- By purchasing single point product solutions (like an application development language or a compiler) an organization pays only for what it uses (versus paying for a complete bundle of applications and tools which it may or may not use). This approach can often be considerably less expensive but it also involves more integration work for the enterprise.

The professional services approach involves finding a services firm that can build and deploy Web services applications for your organization. The upside is that your organization may be able to get products to market more quickly and/or increase the size of its application portfolio very rapidly. The downside is that you may pay top market rates for Web services developers (in other words, it could prove costly).

Another approach that has not yet surfaced but probably will become popular is the ASP approach. Whole enterprises will be able to form their business models around specific industries—and ASPs will be able to build entire specialized application portfolios for these companies using Web services applications automatically found and programmatically integrated over the Internet. Using this approach, businesses will be able to farm out their IT functions and focus specifically on providing services germane to their specific industries.

At present several vendors are fighting for market share in the turnkey application server marketplace. Fewer can be found in the point-product solutions arena, and still fewer in the Web services professional services market segment (so few that in fact this market probably does not exist yet). And no ASPs can yet be found in Web services development and infrastructure provisioning. Still, as this market evolves, competition will arise.

There are no "winners" to declare at present, although IBM is leading the Java-based vendor charge into the application server marketplace, while BEA (the former statistical market leader in terms of number of application server environments sold) is facing very stiff competition from both IBM and now Microsoft.

An issue that goes beyond "market leadership" is that none of us "win" if one vendor has the slickest, bestest, richest implementation of Web services while other vendors have poor implementations. Our goal is to have the majority of information system and software vendors support Web services such that all vendors' systems and software platforms and applications can interoperate with those of other vendors. When this happens, true cross-platform program-to-program communications will be achieved—and we will see our corresponding business models and approaches to computing change forever.

# 9

# Should We Adopt .NET or J2EE?

**A** good place to start when trying to understand the
market positioning of Web services vendors to consider the two dominant approaches to building Web services applications: Microsoft's .NET architecture and the
rest of the industry's Java-based approaches.

There has been a lot of press coverage regarding the battle
between Sun Microsystems and Microsoft Corporation
regarding each company's approach to developing and

deploying Web services. In some respects this "battle" has religious overtones (some application developers are Java language and platform zealots and strongly anti-Microsoft, while others are Microsoft zealots and hold their fellow application developers in equal contempt). Thank goodness there are a lot of people who see the benefits of both approaches!

Web services isn't really about which approach to application development is right or wrong—it is about *cross platform, program-to-program interoperability*. Ultimately, the companies that will be the real winners in the Web services space will be those that make it easiest to develop and deploy robust Web services-based applications that can interoperate with other, disparate application platforms.

This chapter examines the market positioning of J2EE (Java 2 Enterprise Edition) versus .NET. It dispels some myths and clarifies some issues related to each development environment. Further, it provides a basis for business executives to understand why various vendors have chosen to endorse Java or .NET approaches. With this knowledge under your belt, the subsequent chapters on product positioning and on comparative positioning (by vendor) will make a lot more sense.

## Market Dynamics

If you've browsed some recent articles in the popular trade press on the topic of Web services, you may have noticed several common themes:

- The Web services battle is really a Microsoft .NET versus Sun Java event.
- Microsoft has the marketing lead while Sun is having trouble getting its act together.
- Hewlett-Packard is way late to the fray.
- BEA is losing market share to IBM.

Let's take a close look at some of these themes.

## Two Camps: Microsoft .NET and Java

Remember that Web services have been designed to enable applications to work with other applications over the Internet—*regardless of what operating system and program languages each application has been written in.* This being the case, it should matter little which application server platform you build your Web services applications upon. *The whole point of Web services is to enable whatever platform you choose and whatever language you use to work with other, different systems and languages.*

As things stand now, there are two competing approaches to building Web services applications—and that's okay (for consumers and business buyers, choice is a good thing). One approach involves using a Microsoft product suite and the C# language environment on Intel-based platforms, while the other involves using platforms made by Sun, IBM, Hewlett-Packard, Compaq, and other suppliers running the Java programming language.

What are the dynamics of this Sun Java (more specifically Java 2 Enterprise Edition—J2EE) versus Microsoft .NET battle? Is one better than the other? Is one going to dominate the other? From an IT buyer perspective you need to consider that both architectures can get you where you're going from an "application interoperability" point of view. The real story has nothing to do with which approach is better—it has to do with the motives of Sun (and other Java backers like IBM, HP, and Oracle) versus those of Microsoft.

**The J2EE versus .NET Rivalry**

The big picture in this rivalry looks something like this:

- It is commonly believed that he *who controls the application development environment* will be able to capture the hearts and minds of ISV and custom application developers.

- Getting developers committed to building applications using a particular vendor's tools and platform creates a high likelihood that they will not switch platforms or application development environment.

- By ensuring that developers are thus "locked in," vendors increase the probability that their particular systems and development environment will be purchased in the future.

In other words, it is commonly believed that whichever vendor wins the battle of "easy-to-use" development tools, utilities, and add-ons (like automated business process management or personalization) will ultimately sell the most software and (in some cases) related hardware. This "Java versus .NET" battle is really about *capturing the commitment of developers to a particular way of developing applications in order to lock in future sales.* Vendors compete by offering integrated solutions that include systems software (like operating environments and systems management), application development environments, and in some cases related systems hardware, and professional services.

## Opinion

The alleged Microsoft .NET and J2EE battle is nothing more than a pseudodispute—one that matters little to the spirit of what Web services ultimately tries to accomplish (which is cross-platform program-to-program communications). It all ultimately boils down to the following:

> Microsoft is very powerful in the applications development tools marketplace. If competitors allow Microsoft to dominate that market, then competitors end up giving a lot of control over applications development destiny to Microsoft. Ultimately, applications (not hardware characteristics) sell platforms—so allowing Microsoft to control how applications should be developed and deployed could be suicidal for competing platform/operating environment makers.

The Microsoft versus J2EE battle is not really about which approach and which development languages are better. It is really about controlling application development environments in order to *ensure the long-term viability of particular vendors' systems platforms or systems software/application development environment offerings.*

There is, however, one valid aspect to these Microsoft versus Sun articles. Microsoft announced its Visual Studio product (which contains Web services SOAP and other protocols) on February 13, 2002. Sun, on the other hand, has been slower to release its official Web services protocols and registries as part of its Sun ONE offering. Further, IBM offers Web services UDDI, WSDL, and SOAP protocol support as part of its Web-Sphere application server environment. From an analytical perspective Microsoft and IBM appear to be far more aggressive about getting Web services tools and utilities into the hands of developers than Sun.

# Differences Between J2EE and .NET

For those who are particularly interested in the differences between .NET and J2EE, let's take a look at the pros and cons of each development environment from a market-positioning perspective.

A third-party professional services company, the Middleware Company (www.middleware-company.com), recently wrote a white paper that fairly objectively evaluates the differences between .NET and J2EE as development environments. From Middleware's perspective, here are the differences:

## ARGUMENTS SUPPORTING BOTH PLATFORMS

Regardless of which platform you pick, new developers will need to be trained (Java training for J2EE, OO training for .NET).

You can build Web services today using both platforms.

Both platforms offer a low system cost, such as jBoss/Linux/Cobalt for J2EE, or Windows/Win32 hardware for .NET.

Both platforms offer a single-vendor solution.

The scalability of both solutions is theoretically unlimited.

## ARGUMENTS FOR .NET AND AGAINST J2EE

.NET has Microsoft's A-team marketing it.

.NET released their Web services story before J2EE did, and thus has some mind-share.

.NET has a better story for shared context today than J2EE

.NET has an awesome tool story with Visual Studio.NET

.NET has a simpler programming model, enabling rank-and-file developers to be productive without shooting themselves in the foot

.NET gives you language neutrality when developing new eBusiness applications, whereas J2EE makes you treat other languages as separate applications.

.NET benefits from being strongly interweaved with the underlying operating system

## ARGUMENTS FOR J2EE AND AGAINST .NET

J2EE is being marketed by an entire industry.

J2EE is a proven platform, with a few new Web services APIs. .NET is a rewrite and introduces risk as with any first-generation technology.

Only J2EE lets you deploy Web services today.

Existing J2EE code will translate into a J2EE Web services system without major rewrites. Not true for Windows DNA code ported to .NET.

.NET Web services are not interoperable with current industry standards. Their BizTalk framework has proprietary SOAP extensions and does not support ebXML.

J2EE is a more advanced programming model, appropriate for well-trained developers who want to build more advanced object models and take advantage of performance features.

J2EE lets you take advantage of existing hardware you may have.

J2EE gives you platform neutrality, including Windows. You also get good (but not free) portability. This isolates you from heterogeneous deployment environments.

J2EE has a better legacy integration story through the Java Connector Architecture (JCA).

J2EE lets you use any operating system you prefer, such as Windows, UNIX, or mainframe. Developers can use the environment they are most productive in.

*Source:* http://www.theserverside.com/resources/article.jsp?1=J2EE-vs-DOTNET, The Middleware Company. Used by Permission.

Note that *the Middleware Company specializes in Java server-side application deployment*—so many readers may view this commentary as somewhat biased. But, on the whole, it does capture the key points that one should consider when evaluating the .NET approach versus the J2EE approach. It does a fair job of representing the differences between the two approaches as well as representing the commonality between them.

**Microsoft's Response**

At this juncture it is only fair to present Microsoft's perspective on the Middleware Company's white paper. The present section has been derived from a "quite excited" memo on this topic that Microsoft sent to me.

With response to the contention that the BizTalk framework has proprietary SOAP extensions and does not support ebXML—.NET Web services are not currently interoperable with present industry standards. Microsoft asserts that this contention is flat wrong:

- Microsoft is driving standards and is actively promoting compliance both inside and outside the company. Along with IBM, we sponsor periodic interoperability events, inviting ALL Web services stakeholders to take part—on our dime. Is Sun doing this? No. We are fully compliant with SOAP v1.1, WSDL 1.1, UDDI 1.0, XML 1.0, XSLT, HTTP 1.1, XPath, XSD, and many other relevant standards.

Microsoft observed that Sun is not an active participant in SOAPBuilders—the home for Web services interoperability. A quick review of <http://msdn.microsoft.com/library/default.asp?url=/library/enus/dnsrvspec/html/globalxmlWebsrvinterop.asp> will show the state of Web services interoperability efforts.

With respect to the "arguments supporting both platforms" section of the Middleware Company report, Microsoft observed that:

- Regardless of which platform you pick, new developers will need to be trained (Java training for J2EE, OO training for .NET).

With respect to the claim that J2EE supports Web services, Microsoft observed that 600 pages of J2EE specification say nothing at all about Web services, nor do the 700-odd pages of additional specification for JSP, EJB, and the other bits of J2EE. Building Web services "on J2EE" requires a bunch of infrastructure code not included in J2EE and not currently supported by vendors (called variously, "beta" support, "technology preview," third-party libraries). In contrast, .NET is designed from the ground up to support Web services. SOAP, WSDL, and XML are intrinsic to the .NET platform and the .NET tools. "We have customers who are using this stuff in production, today. There's a clear difference here."

Microsoft agreed that both platforms offer a low system cost, such as jBoss/Linux/Cobalt for J2EE, or Windows/Win32 hardware for .NET.

With respect to the statement, "You can build Web services today using both platforms," Microsoft observed that .NET was designed as a platform for Web services. J2EE has Web services bolted on as an afterthought. On .NET, Web services—SOAP and WSDL—are easy to create, easy to consume and easy to deploy. The same is not true on J2EE.

With response to the Middleware company's "Arguments for .NET and against J2EE" Microsoft observed that:

- .NET has Microsoft's A-team marketing it.
- An unfounded opinion such as this is irrelevant in the comparison of two platforms.
- .NET released their Web services story before J2EE did, and thus has some mind-share.
- .NET has a better story for shared context today than J2EE.
- .NET has an awesome tool story with Visual Studio.NET.
- .NET has a simpler programming model, enabling rank-and-file developers to be productive without shooting themselves in the foot.
- .NET gives you language neutrality when developing new eBusiness applications, whereas J2EE makes you treat other languages as separate applications.
- .NET benefits from being strongly interweaved with the underlying operating system.

Microsoft further stated that the authors of the Middleware Company's report failed to note the key advantages of .NET:

- .NET is designed specifically to support Web services, at all points in the network: servers, clients, devices. J2EE does not have the broad reach of .NET. It focuses on Web services only on the server side. It ignores the huge potential of Web services at the edges of tomorrow's intelligent network.

- .NET is designed with rocket-fast performance in mind. In contrast, J2EE focuses more on the academic pursuit of OO purity, with consequent costs in performance.

- .NET is much more secure than any off-the-shelf J2EE offering today. Digital signatures for code, real code versioning, secure downloadable modules—J2EE has none of these key capabilities for security.

Microsoft also observed that J2EE does not integrate Web services into the platform and attempts to blur the line between Web services—SOAP and WSDL based—and its legacy object protocols (RMI/CORBA) to get some of promise of Web services to rub off on its own cumbersome implementation.

Further, in the "Arguments for J2EE and against .NET" section, Microsoft took issue with the statement that "J2EE is being marketed by an entire industry":

- The J2EE "industry" is in trouble. None of the standard bearers are making any money. BEA is the strongest vendor—they have just posted a loss on declining revenues. Every other J2EE app server vendor is losing money on shrinking revenues (Iona, Silverstream, Gemstone, Persistence, ATG, Macromedia), and their stock share prices are way down, some 85% or more. Many are refocusing their strategies (Silverstream, Persistence, ATG, Gemstone, others), in search of a sustainable business. The J2EE ecosystem of software companies is in terrible shape.

With respect to the argument that "J2EE is a proven platform, with a few new Web services APIs. .NET is a rewrite and introduces risk as with any first-generation technology," Microsoft observed that:

- True, J2EE is proven. But proven as what? It is proven to be expensive (see Gartner's recent claim that companies have overspent $1B on J2EE kit they do not use). It is proven to be slow (see www.gotdotnet.com/team/compare). It is proven to be hard to program (see the code complexity in the J2EE Blueprint called "Pet Store"). It is proven to be incomplete and insufficient (lack of Web services, poor support for XML, no disconnected model, poor code versioning, many other examples).

With respect to the statement "Only J2EE lets you deploy Web services today" Microsoft stated:

- Not true, or otherwise a very misleading statement. See my comments above: J2EE includes no support for Web services. Crediting J2EE with Web services support is wrong. Customers have to "integrate it themselves" and the vendors aren't supporting it anyway.

With regard to the statement that "existing J2EE code will translate into a J2EE Web services system without major rewrites" Microsoft responded:

- Not true for Windows DNA code ported to .NET. Windows DNA code can very easily be exposed as SOAP-accessible services with the MS SOAP Toolkit, which was the first production-quality SOAP engine released by any vendor. There is no need to rewrite anything to .NET. Likewise, there is no need to rewrite J2EE apps to expose them as Web services. The situations are very similar.

On the statement "J2EE is a more advanced programming model, appropriate for well-trained developers who want to build more advanced object models and take advantage of performance features" Microsoft issued a qualified "no complaint." Here's the response:

- No complaint here, if by "advanced" they mean "complicated." As for performance, check out www.gotdotnet.com/team/compare—this is a pretty strong indication that .NET applications perform significantly better than J2EE applications. In fact, two years after J2EE was originally released, there is STILL NO EVIDENCE that J2EE delivers competitive performance, or even reasonable performance, as compared to the Microsoft platform. See TPC-C, TPC-W, see any other independent benchmark—none include J2EE.

To the statement that "J2EE lets you take advantage of existing hardware you may have" Microsoft responded:

- Presumably this is an advantage, because J2EE will run on Sparc or RS6000, while Windows and .NET will not. This is true, and also irrelevant for most commercial ventures. Server hardware has a half-life of 2–3 years, according to Moore's Law, with the understanding that servers tend to live longer than desktops. It makes no business sense to recycle server hardware for newly developed apps. Server hardware probably represents 10% or less of the overall system cost for an enterprise application. This potential cost savings is a wash, when considered with the increased software cost of J2EE (see my comments above).

Microsoft next evaluated the claim that "J2EE gives you platform neutrality, including Windows. You also get good (but not free) portability. This isolates you from heterogeneous deployment environments."

- There is little actual business value here, for enterprises and users of this infrastructure. Do customers often "port" their applications from Solaris to AIX in mid life? or vice versa? No. In fact, the portability of J2EE is possibly its greatest weakness, because (a) the portability is not real, and (b) it conversely exacts a real cost in terms of capability and performance. Building a portable platform means customers cannot take advantage of platform-specific optimizations, like transaction coordinators, resource coordinators, failover, and so on (think of all the special services in Windows Server, or in IBM's zOS), UNLESS they do so in a nonportable fashion.

With respect to the view that "J2EE has a better legacy integration story through the Java ConnectorArchitecture (JCA)" Microsoft responded:

- This is utterly false. JCA is "paper and vapor." Where are the shipping connectors? Where are the reference customers? Microsoft has real customers using our host integration server, with great performance and transactional integrity. We've got 100+ Biztalk connectors today (though it is true we did not have this list of connectors at the time this opinion piece was originally written, in July).

On the topic "J2EE lets you use any operating system you prefer, such as Windows, UNIX, or mainframe. Developers can use the environment they are most productive in" Microsoft responded:

- Yes, Productivity is the issue. But the OS doesn't affect programmer productivity nearly as much as rich, solid, easy-to-use tools, with intuitive user interfaces. This is Microsoft's strength, as even the authors of the paper acknowledge. VisualStudio.NET makes all the difference for programmer productivity.

Finally, Microsoft suggested that for those interested in tracking the state of Web services interoperability, a good site to visit for further information is: http://msdn.microsoft.com/library/default.asp?url=/library/enus/dnsrvspec/html/globalxmlWebsrvinterop.asp.

A discussion about which platform is better for Web services (Java or .NET) can get quite heated. And developers from both camps can get equally excited about their respective positions. This author's advice is to remember that ultimately Web services will help eliminate cross-platform and cross-development language program-to-program communications disputes. This will cool off the discussions about which is better.

# Chapter Summary

Again, it is important to remember that the purpose of Web services is to foster cross-platform program-to-program communications. *Interoperability*, not the choice of development-language environment, is what is important in Web services.

Why do people choose one language approach over the other? In the case of Java, there is a promise that Java-language programs can be written on one platform environment and easily moved to another. (This promise is sometimes fulfilled, depending upon the application's complexity and whether the application took advantage of custom extensions on the originating platform that may or may not be available on the target platform.) In the case of Microsoft, cross-platform program transportability is not featured. When you write to .NET, you are writing programs that will run in a Windows-only environment (but thanks to Web services, these programs will interoperate with other programs, including Java-based programs, quite readily).

In choosing a .NET or Java development environment, business executives and application developers should look closely at:

- The breadth and depth of the development environment your vendor offers (with extensions for application compilation, business process integration, security, and other integrated add-ons);
- The availability of the key Web services protocols and services you need (such as UDDI registries and WSDL/SOAP protocols);
- The skill set of your existing development organization; and
- The computer-systems mix in your existing IT infrastructure.

Remember, too, that in a world where one vendor claims to have implemented Web services protocols and directories while another vendor has not implemented them, nobody wins. Being a market leader with early implementations does little to provide the wide-ranging interoperability between vendors that Web services is all about. Only when the major vendors all support Web services protocols and directories does the IT buyer really win—because at that point cross-platform program-to-program communications is assured.

A lot of confusing information can be found in news articles and on Web sites, portraying the forthcoming Web services battles as being between Microsoft and Sun. In fact, the real battles will be fought between Microsoft (with its Visual Studio suite of Web services development products) and companies that offer similar tools using the Java development language. What this means is that Web services buyers will be making choices based on:

1. The completeness of the Web services product suites (language environments, development tools, and additional tools and utilities that help create complete Web services solutions); and,

2. The actual language of choice (Microsoft will be pushing the C# language—all the remaining competitors will be pushing J2EE Java language approach).

Choosing an appropriate Web services approach does not necessitate a Microsoft versus Sun battle. It's an applications and development tools battle that will be won by the companies that offer the best integrated product suites for easily and completely building and deploying Web services based solutions.

# 10

# Vendor Comparison— Contrasting Various Product and Service Offerings

**In This Chapter:**

- A discussion of various, randomly chosen vendors that offer Web services products and services
- Vendors "profiled"
  - The three approaches described earlier will be illustrated using key vendors as examples
  - Category 1: Application server providers
    - Example 1: Turnkey application servers
      - Application server hardware/software/service providers
        - IBM (WebSphere), and Sun (ONE)
    - Example 2: Application server software (and sometimes service) providers
      - Microsoft (.NET) is described
      - Other suppliers, including IONA, Web Methods, Vitria, SeeBeyond, Tibco, Silverstream, Lucin, CapeClear, Crossworlds, Velocigen, Savvion, and ASPAlliance.com, fit in this category but are not covered.
  - Category 2: Building your own a la carte, point product Web services applications

- Example 1: Point product tools and utilities
- Example 2: Open-source Apache server
- Category 3: Professional services firms that can help your organization build and maintain Web services applications

**Key Insights:**
- There are several ways to go about implementing Web services. This chapter looks closely at several suppliers of Web services products and services.

How should your organization compare, contrast, and differentiate the product and service offerings of various Web services vendors? This chapter gives you a basic understanding of the product offerings of various Web services vendors. It does not focus on picking or portraying winners or losers. As stated previously, having one major vendor with a superior one implementation of Web services and another with an inferior one does not yield the result that we are all looking for—cross-platform program-to-program interoperability. Instead, this chapter examines how multiple vendors have structured their respective product offerings, so that you, a business executive, will understand where to turn to purchase the hardware, software, and/or services needed to build your own Web services environment.

Chapter 8 described three approaches to building a Web services architecture: (1) turnkey application servers, (2) a la carte Web services tools/utilities, and (3) professional services firms. This chapter examines vendors in each of these categories.

## Category 1: Application Server Providers

Application server providers are divided into two classes: (1) providers of turnkey platforms, and (2) providers of software-based application development environments.

**Example 1: Turnkey Platform Providers**

The complete turnkey platform vendors covered in this section include:

- Hewlett Packard (with its Bluestone/Netaction product offerings);
- IBM (with its WebSphere application server and accompanying value-add products for systems management, security, and other infrastructure elements, plus its additional business process management and personalization software);
- Sun (with its ONE application server product set, its iPlanet Application Server, and its Forte 4GL application development environment).

These vendors offer hardware, application development software, and related professional services—in other words, turnkey platforms. Especially noteworthy are IBM and Sun, because they are expected to be major influences in the Web services market over time. Hewlett Packard (HP) is also interesting because the company has rapidly assembled a complete application server environment (Netaction) and is poised to compete favorably with Sun (and some day with IBM). The efforts of some of the other major second-tier application server vendors (Compaq, Dell, and Unisys) are not covered here, but they resemble in many respects what HP is doing to become a major player in the turnkey application server marketplace.

Note that BEA and Microsoft are not covered in this section. They provide application server software, not turnkey application servers. But Microsoft is covered in the next section.

**Vendor Profile: IBM**

**Market Positioning**  IBM has three solid advantages in seeking to dominate the market in Web services application server provisioning.

1. IBM has probably the most potent arsenal of application server products and services, and it is rapidly gaining market share in the application server market space (see the subsection on "Product/Service Offerings");

2. IBM has a strong strategic commitment to Web services application development, as evidenced by its heavy participation in W3C standards committees, and

3. IBM is the first major turnkey platform provider to provide access to UDDI registry and program-to-program application development tools.

IBM has understood early the strategic importance of Web services and has built what is arguably the industry's most potent turnkey application server platform—complete with the hardware, software, and services needed to build next-generation Web services applications.

As of this writing, IBM has overtaken market leader BEA in terms of units sold in the application server marketplace.

The WebSphere product line has been experiencing stunning growth at a time when the IT industry is in a lull. And being in the Web services market early will likely prove a strong advantage to IBM over time. Application developers and business managers are already turning to WebSphere as a "product of choice" for building Web services enabled applications, and they will probably stick with IBM over the long term rather than switch platforms unnecessarily.

**Product/Service Offerings**   A high-level view finds IBM's WebSphere application server environment to be rich in basic application development software as well as value-added software that improves infrastructure (security, reliability, manageability) and enables business process reengineering.

WebSphere:

- Runs across its four hardware platforms, which include its mainframe, e-Series (AS/400), UNIX (RS-6000), and Windows hardware platforms;
- Includes a myriad of tools and utilities designed to help developers build Java language based applications;
- Offers tools for Web design, presentation, personalization, portal creation, voice support, and publishing;
- Offers tools to assist in business process reengineering, policy management, and the development of business rules and workflow;

- Offers numerous products that enable connection to and messaging with legacy system environments (to allow for cross-platform integration);
- Offers products that enable e-commerce and B2B integration; and
- Offers infrastucture extensions that allow for greater systems manageability and security than many other application server product offerings.

On the professional services side of the house, IBM has a Web services specialist organization (known as the jStart) that can (selectively) help prospective Web services users develop Web services solutions. (Many of the examples used in Chapter 7, "Real World Web Services Examples," actually contracted with IBM's J-team for help and advice in designing and deploying their Web services applications.) The jStart team offers training, advice, mentoring, and development support to early-adopters of Web services architecture.

**Competitive Positioning** The Web services marketplace will ultimately shape up as a battle between Java language based application server makers and .NET environment supporters. Each approach has its strengths and weaknesses—but, if past purchasing behavior holds true, most enterprises will prefer to standardize on one approach as they build their applications portfolios and developer expertise.

In this either/or scenario IBM is perched as the broadest and deepest choice for Java-based application development and deployment today. Other Java-based Web services suppliers have a fair amount of catching up to do, both in the depth and breath of their product offerings and in the provisioning of professional services. So, in the short term, IBM can be regarded as the leader-of-the-Java-pack.

But if the rest of the Java pack is lagging behind IBM in terms of breadth and depth, which companies really are IBM's primary competitors? The real competition is from the alternative solution provider—Microsoft.

The Microsoft .NET approach is distinctly different from the IBM WebSphere approach. .NET is an application development environment that is built for Intel platforms and will largely be sold by third-party systems suppliers or directly by Microsoft. Those third parties will garner license revenue commissions as well as revenue from the sale of related professional services. By contrast, WebSphere is a highly integrated platform that will drive not only hardware and software revenue for IBM and its business partners but also related professional services revenue.

Each company has a different go-to-market approach and different revenue models—but it is amazing how similar their product structure and Web services architectures really are. Each company supports XML, UDDI, WSDL, and SOAP. Each offers very rich application development environments rife with tools and utilities that streamline the job of writing and compiling applications. Further, each company's product suite has value-added software that allows for business process reengineering, for improved messaging, for varied device connection, for personalization, and a dozen other similarities.

Early in 2002 it seemed likely that during the first half of the year IBM's primary Web services competition would come from Microsoft, but in the second half, the other Java-based turnkey platform competitors would be able to put forward platforms that will compete better with IBM. Ultimately, though, this market will really be a battle between Microsoft .NET and Java-based platforms—with major victories going to the vendors that make the easiest-to-use integrated application development environments for Web services.

**IBM Summary**    IBM is sitting in a highly enviable position in the application server marketplace. The company was the first turnkey platform supplier to officially release Web services application development products, tools, and utilities. And it has a very rich, deep, and highly integrated suite of ancillary products and services that enable enterprises not only to build Web services but also to streamline business processes, incorporate the use of intelligent portable devices, and much, much more.

Being first out of the blocks can be a good thing if the company is able to capture the hearts and minds of a large portion of the Java development community, because the likelihood of this community moving to new platforms down the road diminishes as IBM's WebSphere gets stronger and stronger. Being first means nothing at all, though, if the other industry leaders are slow to introduce their Web services products— because being the best and only show in town does not foster *cross-platform* program-to-program interoperability.

Still, if you are an IT buyer and you are looking for a completely integrated suite of Java development tools with which to develop Web services applications today—IBM is the one place to turn for the most comprehensive set of hardware, software, and services offerings available.

**Vendor Profile: Sun**

**Market Position** In the Java world Sun Microsystems has a lot going for it. The company created Java, and the company's professional services organization has a huge commitment to fostering the growth of Java-based applications. Java is strategically important to Sun. Add the fact that Sun servers are the market leaders in the enterprise UNIX server marketplace, and the words "Sun" and "Java servers" should go hand-in-hand—right?

How is Sun positioned in the Web services marketplace? Succinctly, and in the company's own words, Sun is positioned as follows:

Sun believes that businesses want an IT infrastructure that supports their current computing environment, while providing a platform that prepares them for future Web-based services. Sun offers many resources to help businesses create Services on Demand, including field-proven reference architectures, market-leading products, and worldwide professional services. Services on Demand can help businesses create a sustainable business advantage by leveraging the Internet to help maximize IT investments, minimize time to market, create new market opportunities, and reduce overall costs.

The key is the Sun™ Open Net Environment (Sun ONE), Sun's vision, architecture, platform, and expertise to enable the Services on Demand of today and tomorrow.

*Source:* http://www.sun.com/software/sunone/wp-getstarted/. Used by Permission.

In short, Sun is positioned to compete with other Web services competitors as a provider of Web services enabled application servers. Its revenue stream is derived from the sale of hardware and systems software—as well as from the sale of related professional services.

**Product Offerings**    Sun's Web services strategy is manifest in its Open Net Environment (ONE) initiative. This initiative pulls together all of the application development tools and utilities, the ancillary applications such as security and management, and the value-added applications such as business process reengineering and personalization—all into a single unified architecture.

The three main product sets that make up the Sun ONE platform are:

- IPlanet;
- Forte (a toolset for building distributed applications); and
- Solaris (Sun's UNIX Operating Environment)

Let's take a closer look at these environments.

IPlanet, a joint venture "product wing" between Sun and various business partners, provides Web and application services, commerce services, communication services, user management, integration, and portal services for the Sun ONE architecture. With respect to Web services, it has an XML-enabled integration broker that allows for the creation of new Web services applications as well as the integration of legacy applications. It also contains business process management software that allows applications to be optimized with business processes. At this juncture, iPlanet supports SOAP rev 1.1, SML/HTTP and JMS-based message transport, and LDAP (lightweight directory access protocol) as opposed to UDDI (UDDI will come later).

Forte is the application development environment used to build Web services (and many other application types). In fact, the Forte development environment supports Java, C++, Fortran/HPC, TeamWare, and C language environments. As the creator of Java, Sun's implementation is excellent. Sun's Java tools are found packaged in Forte application development software offerings.

The final element of Sun ONE's architecture is the company's own Solaris environment. This operating environment is quite mature and consists of a UNIX kernel with substantial improvements in the areas of scalability, reliability, availability, and manageability.

**Competitive Positioning**   Many articles in the trade contend that Sun has been slow to respond to the challenge of bringing Web services application development environments to market. Despite the fact that the company does offer XML, WSDL, and SOAP as part of its iPlanet integration server, a continuing theme in the press is that Sun is behind Microsoft and others in Web services application provisioning.

This Sun-is-behind argument can be refuted as follows:

1. The company has a complete application server environment in place today with the combination of its Forte application development tools, its iPlanet integration server, and its operating environment extensions (security, reliability, etc.).

2. Remember, the Gartner Group prediction (illustrated in the introductory section of this book) indicates that Web services products will start to move into the mainstream (circa 2004) as UDDI matures. Sun will build its Web services reference base and provide further product integration well in advance of 2004.

3. The company has been very actively participating in XML, SOAP, and UDDI standards development. Its knowledge of the Web services specifications, its strong UNIX market position, and its influence on Java language development and deployment will most assuredly make Sun a strong contender in the Web services application server marketplace.

4. The same kind of argument that Sun-is-behind was once made in the UNIX enterprise server marketplace—and that argument, too, proved false. Sun is now the leader in UNIX enterprise server sales.

Given these counterarguments, and the Gartner Group projections that the Web services marketplace will not really start to mature until UDDI starts to take off in late 2004, this author does not believe that Sun is "behind" in building Web services product and service offerings.

**Sun Summary**    As noted earlier in this book, there are almost religious overtones in discussions of which approach to application development is better—the Java approach or the .NET approach. Sun is a pure Java player and has the products and services in place to compete effectively in the Web services application server marketplace.

One major perception among the press and some members of the analyst community is that Sun is late to market. More accurately, Sun was late to articulate its strategy—but its products and services will be aligned to meet market needs as Web services gain market acceptance.

**Example 2: Application Server Software Providers**

The two major players building the *software environments* that drive application servers are BEA and Microsoft. But dozens of other companies also have application development environments, tools, and utilities that also legitimately fit into this software/server category. Among them are: IONA, Web Methods, Vitria, SeeBeyond, Tibco, Silverstream, Lucin, CapeClear, Crossworlds, Velocigen, Savvion, and Actional. IONA has been randomly chosen to represent this bunch.

All of these vendors provide application development software environments—and many of those can run across multiple systems platforms. Many of the vendors had origins in the Enterprise Application Integration (EAI) marketplace and are now looking to segue into the Web services applications server marketplace. Some of them make their money by providing software solutions only, while others sell both software and services. None of them make their money by selling hardware (for that aspect of the business they rely on business partnerships with hardware makers and value-added resellers).

This section covers the market, product, and competitive positioning of Microsoft.

Microsoft

**Market Positioning**  Microsoft believes strongly that the computing world is moving toward a Web services-based application model, and it has been extremely aggressive in building market awareness of Web services. The company believes that Web services will alter the way that applications are designed, built, and delivered—and is leading the charge toward this new way of doing business.

At present, to help build Web services momentum, Microsoft's approach is to go after the development community with:

1. A suite of easy-to-use application development tools.
2. Value-added software (for automating business processes, for instance).
3. A Windows 2000 operating system that has been improved to help compensate for some of the current shortcoming of Web services standards (in the areas of security, manageability, and reliability, for instance).

The company's goal is to help populate the marketplace with Web services applications that make use of Microsoft's own .NET architecture (explained later in this section).

To make things easier for developers, Microsoft's .NET environment contains:

- A rich application development environment (under the product name Visual Studio);
- A focus on making Web services enabling its Windows 2000, SQL Server, and Exchange Server environments, while also focusing on building a rich suite of value-added integration and business process management tools (as part of its BizTalk application server environment);
- A focus on creating "building-block" infrastructure components that will make it easy for consumers and users to move from one computing environment to another. These building-block services also make it easier for developers to concentrate on writing appli-

cations, as opposed to dealing with infrastructure plumbing in order to make their applications work properly in a distributed computing environment;

- A focus on creating "immersive" human-interface environments on various types of platforms (PCs, PDAs, handheld computers, tablets, and other to-be-invented devices); and,

- A focus on making the user's experience simple and compelling.

**Microsoft's .NET Strategy**   Microsoft's overarching plan for Web services is manifest in its .NET architecture. What is .NET? According to Sanjay Parthasarathy, Vice President of Platform Strategy at Microsoft, the following definition represents an easy way to understand .NET:

SIDEBAR 10-1
## THE SIMPLEST WAY TO DEFINE .NET

The best way to define .NET is to think about what .NET is going to do. Microsoft believes a silent shift to distributed computing is happening. Over the last couple of years, people have been laying fat pipes to the point where bandwidth is a lot less limited than it has been in the past. Combined with the Moore's Law effect, where the processing power doubles every 18 months and the prices are halved, you now have the option to do really distributed computing for the first time: because bandwidth is less expensive, you can do the processing wherever it is most optimal.

There are lots of examples of such distributed applications today. Napster is an application that uses a rich client talking to a directory service in the cloud, and uses all of the participating computers on the network as servers. Another example of a distributed application is instant messaging, where you have a rich client that talks to a buddy list in the cloud and communicates with other rich clients—Instant Messenger and Windows—in the network.

So .NET is aimed at accelerating this next generation of distributed computing.

### THREE LEVERS

We believe there are three levers to pull to make this distributed computing generation happen as fast as it can:

1. Web services: The first lever is that everything needs to be a Web service. This applies to both pieces of software and resources in the network like storage.

2. Aggregation and integration: The second lever that needs to be pulled is that once you have these Web services, you need to be able to aggregate and integrate these Web services in very simple and easy ways.

3. Simple and compelling user experience: The third lever to accelerate distributed computing is you need to have a simple and compelling consumer or end user experience.

So those three levers we think are essential to accelerating this move to distributed computing:

- Everything is a Web service;

- The ability to aggregate and integrate Web services; and

- The ability to deliver a simple and compelling experience to end users.

.NET is really aimed at pulling these levers to accelerate the move to distributed computing, and we're doing five things in .NET to pull these levers right.

*Source:* http://www.microsoft.com/Partner/Products/MicrosoftNet/ MicrosoftNETDefined.asp. Used by Permission.

Notice how important Microsoft believes Web services are. They are central to building next-generation applications; to be successful they will require a lot of integration work (and Microsoft builds tools for this kind of application integration); and ultimately they need to be able to deliver a simple, satisfying, and compelling user experience.

**Product Positioning**  Like those of other application server makers, Microsoft's products consist of application development environment tools and utilities, value-added software to automate business processes or to help build Web sites more effectively, and platform extensions to help optimize Intel-based hardware and the Windows operating environment for Web services. More specifically, Microsoft offers:

1. Visual Studio as its C++ application development environment.

2. BizTalk server for business process reengineering and management.

3. A whole range of software extensions that help make the Windows 2000 operating system more reliable,

manageable, scalable, and secure (in order to augment Web services application servers).

From an *application development* perspective, Microsoft's .NET architecture offers the following:

Common Language Runtime (CLR) and .NET Framework.

Unified programming model.

More component "building-blocks" for writing less code.

Ability to target multiple devices.

Rich XML data—ADO.NET.

Industry-leading tools support.

[Future], Windows .NET Server offers developers the opportunity to improve productivity by enabling them to use multiple programming languages and native XML Web services. In addition, the industry's most productive tools allow one programming model to be used for clients, servers, and devices that enable the Microsoft vision of information anywhere, on any device. The Microsoft Visual Basic® and Visual C++® development systems as well as third-party tools and applications easily integrate with Microsoft Visual Studio .NET.

*Source:* http://msdn.microsoft.com/library/default.asp?url=/library/enus/dnnetserv/html/windowsnetserver.asp. Used by Permission.

From a business integration perspective, Microsoft adds value to its .NET application server environment with its BizTalk server. What is BizTalk Server?

BizTalk Server 2000 enables you to rapidly build and deploy integrated business processes within your organization and with your trading partners. You can get your solutions to market quicker and use fewer resources so that you can move swiftly to respond to your customers' needs and competitive pressures.

BizTalk Server 2000 offers a suite of tools and services that make building business processes and integrating applications fundamentally faster. You can quickly implement secure, reliable trading partner relationships independent of operating systems, programming models, or programming languages.

## BUILD DYNAMIC BUSINESS PROCESSES

The BizTalk Server infrastructure helps you to quickly integrate, manage, and automate dynamic business processes by exchanging business documents among applications within or across organizational boundaries. With all of the tools companies need for business process orchestration, BizTalk Server helps you build processes that span not only applications, but also businesses, over the Internet. Graphical tools make it easy for business analysts and application developers to model and implement solutions for your business.

### EASILY INTEGRATE APPLICATIONS AND BUSINESS PARTNERS

BizTalk Server 2000 makes it easy for developers to integrate applications and businesses. Business analysts and application developers benefit from a host of rich graphical tools for building XML schemas, performing schema transformations, establishing trading partner relationships over the Internet, and tracking and analyzing data and documents that are exchanged. With support for XML and standard Internet technologies, BizTalk Server 2000 extends the features of traditional e-commerce and electronic data interchange (EDI) to entire e-commerce communities.

### ENSURE INTEROPERABILITY BY USING PUBLIC STANDARDS

With extensive support for public standards and specifications such as XML, EDI, and HTTP, and with security standards such as public key encryption and digital signatures, BizTalk Server 2000 ensures the highest level of interoperability and security with your applications and business partners.

*Source:* http://www.microsoft.com/biztalk/evaluation/overview/2000/default.asp. Used by Permission.

Finally, from a platform perspective, Microsoft's .NET architecture is easily integrated with the Windows operating system and with other Microsoft platform servers, such as its Internet Information Server (IIS) and its messaging platforms. This integration makes it easy for developers to deploy and integrate newly written Web services applications on Microsoft Windows based servers, and it allows developers to take advantage of Microsoft extensions that allow for performance tuning, scalability, and improved manageability:

.NET Framework integration with the operating system means you don't have to deploy the .NET Framework separately.

Code access security works in conjunction with Software Restriction Policies to give you more control for fighting hostile code.

Microsoft Message Queue (MSMQ) supports SOAP as a native protocol.

Existing COM+ applications can be automatically converted into Web services with no new code.

ASP.NET integration with the IIS 6.0 process model.

Increased performance.

Better scalability.

Lowest TCO [total cost of ownership].

*Source:* http://msdn.microsoft.com/library/default.asp?url=/library/enus/dnnetserv/html/windowsnetserver.asp. Used by Permission.

**.NET My Services**   Most of Microsoft's competitors talk about "improving the user experience," because Web services also allow a new way to build personalized applications that can provide "valet" programmatic requests for users. But Microsoft is actually bringing to market these valet services in the form of .NET My Services.

What kinds of services can common, everyday users of the Internet expect to see from Microsoft? Here are some examples:

- **.NET Profile.** Name, nickname, special dates, picture, address.
- **.NET Contacts.** Electronic relationships/address book.
- **.NET Locations.** Electronic and geographical location and rendezvous.
- **.NET Alerts.** Alert subscription, management, and routing.
- **.NET Presence.** Online, offline, busy, free, which device(s) to send alerts to.
- **.NET Inbox.** Inbox items like e-mail and voice mail, including existing mail systems.
- **.NET Calendar.** Time and task management.
- **.NET Documents.** Raw document storage.
- **.NET ApplicationSettings.** Application settings.
- **.NET FavoriteWebSites.** Favorite URLs and other Web identifiers.
- **.NET Wallet.** Receipts, payment instruments, coupons, and other transaction records.

- **.NET Devices.** Device settings, capabilities.
- **.NET Services.** Services provided for an identity.
- **.NET Lists.** General-purpose lists.
- **.NET Categories.** A way to group lists.

www.microsoft.com/myservices/services/userexperi-
ences.asp

Technically, .NET My Services are Web services based applications that use XML based messages and SOAP protocols.
Programs written using .NET My Services enable users to
manage their calendars, describe locations where they can
be contacted, manage profile information (such as name,
address, credit card numbers for electronic purchases), and
even allow users to log on once to access many different
types of systems (eliminating the problem of having to
remember multiple passwords and user names).

.NET My Services warranted special mention in this section,
because few Microsoft competitors at this point have actually extended their Web services reach to individuals,
choosing instead to concentrate on Web services for enterprise application development and deployment. Microsoft
is approaching the market from the top level (enterprise)
and the bottom level (individual users).

Note: Despite the fact that .NET My Services is being re-
evaluated, the concept is still viable.

**Competitive Positioning**   Chapter 8 discussed how
Microsoft is positioned to compete with dozens of Java language and development environment proponents.

In short, Microsoft's .NET strategy is based on using Web services protocols and registries, enhancing them with extensions for security, manageability, reliability (and other
"abilities"), and integrating Web services applications with
other Microsoft server environments (such as BizTalk, IIS, and
messaging) to create a robust application server environment.

The elements of this application server environment are the
same as those of HP, IBM, Sun, and others: application
development tools and utilities; value-added software for
integration with other business applications and infrastructure elements; and platform tuning.

On a technology level, the primary difference between Microsoft and its Java competitors is that Microsoft focuses its support on C# and Basic languages while its competitors obviously focus on Java. (But note: Microsoft and its competitors also support Web services communications with other language environments.)

Also, Microsoft's approach to the market differs from that of hardware makers like IBM and Sun, in that Microsoft makes a software environment that can be sold on various vendors' Windows-based Intel platforms (whereas IBM's WebSphere is focused on IBM platforms and Sun's ONE is focused on Sun's Solaris-based UNIX architecture). Microsoft leaves almost all of the professional services revenue to its business partners (whereas IBM and Sun focus on professional services as a source of revenue).

**Microsoft Summary**    The goal of Web services is to foster cross-platform program-to-program communications. Microsoft believes that the best languages to use are C-based (C++ or C#) or Visual Basic. Other suppliers believe that the best language/middleware approach is Java language based. Despite this basic difference, major competing platforms all look strangely alike. They all have personalization software, business process management software, Web services protocol support (promised or real), and platform extensions to improve reliability, security, and so on.

What Microsoft is doing with .NET differs notably in the area of personal services. Microsoft .NET My Services delivers what other vendors are only talking about—personal valet services (programs that can offload individuals from certain mundane tasks). In this area Microsoft is showing creativity that many suppliers lack.

Also encouraging is Microsoft's strong participation on Web services standards committees. With Microsoft and all of the major Java suppliers backing Web services, this form of distributed computing will finally (at last) become a reality.

IONA
Technologies
PLC

**Market Positioning** IONA Technologies is yet another example of a software company that makes a Web application server development environment that can be used to help build Web services applications. Additionally, IONA makes revenue selling its consulting and educational services.

What is IONA? The following (excerpted from IONA's Web site) is a brief description of the company and its market position.

IONA's story began in 1983 in the computer science department of Trinity College in Dublin where the company's founders spent much of a decade researching the ability to make computers, and the software that runs them, work together collaboratively. In 1993, IONA shipped its *ORBIX* product, which enables distributed computers and software systems to work together collaboratively. IONA left the Trinity College campus and began opening offices around the world. In 1995, the company opened its U.S. headquarters in Boston. Two years later, IONA "went public" on the NASDAQ exchange, in what was then the 5th largest software IPO ever. Currently, IONA employs more than 900 people in 30 offices worldwide, generating in excess of $180 million in annual revenue and has been profitable every year since its foundation.

In recent years, changes in the business and computing world have played favorably to IONA's strengths. From a consumer perspective, e-business enables people to get the information, goods and services they want from the world's computers to their own computers at home. From a corporate perspective, the e-business revolution enables companies and their suppliers, partners and respective customers to exchange goods and services online. In each case, the world's computer systems must be interconnected for them to work together—the very idea IONA was created to address.

*Source:* Excerpted from http://www.iona.com/info/aboutus/. Used by Permission.

**Product Positioning** IONA's Orbix E2A Application Server Platform is available in three editions: (1) the *Collaborate Edition*, which focuses on providing a suite of process integration solutions that allow IONA customers to build collaborative solutions inside an enterprise and externally to business partners; (2) the *Partner Edition*, which provides a Web connector between trading partners that have deployed the Collaborate Edition; and (3) the *XMLBus Edition* (the development platform for "pure" Web services).

The following is an in-depth description of IONA's XMLBus Edition (E2A is IONA's "End-2-Anywhere" architecture"):

## IONA's END-2-ANYWHERE WEB SERVICES POSITIONING

Orbix E2A XMLBus Edition is IONA's entry-level solution for the construction and integration of Web services. This rich environment enables developers to easily implement, deploy, secure, access, test, integrate, and manage standards-based Web services. XMLBus Edition is built on a foundation of open standards including XML, SOAP, WSDL, and UDDI, providing interoperability among distinct programming paradigms such as J2EE, CORBA, and .NET. IONA's patent-pending Web services Container provides a consistent and simple model for Web service development and deployment across Java, J2EE and CORBA environments.

### WHO SHOULD USE THIS PRODUCT

- Companies that wish to expose specific information assets as Web services
- Companies or developers that wish to build and deploy new Web services or connect with existing ones
- Companies or developers that want to host Web services
- Companies or developers that want to educate themselves on how to build, deploy and manage Web services

### BENEFITS

- Seamless upgrade to Orbix E2A Collaborate Edition for a comprehensive Web Services Integration Platform
- Build a service-oriented architecture with components built on disparate programming paradigms such as Java, J2EE, .NET, COM, and CORBA
- Create new avenues into existing data and new faces into existing services
- Leverage existing IT investments and quickly build Web services without writing new code
- Leverage existing J2EE environment for runtime control, clustering, and security of Web services
- Easy-to-use interface gives developers the tools they need to get started building Web services, TODAY
- Developers can aggregate and combine functionality in new and innovative ways
- Unique Web services container simplifies development and deployment of Web services

## FEATURES

- Provides a non-programmatic, graphical environment for defining, assembling, and integrating Web services from existing resources (Java, J2EE, and CORBA)

- Provides tools to create new Web services

- Generates proxy-based and J2ME-ready Web Service client applications

- Built on open standards including XML, SOAP, WSDL, UDDI, and HTTP(S)

- Enables remote procedure calls and direct XML document exchange between business services or programs

- Secure communication through TLS/SSL

- Web Services Container can run standalone or be deployed into existing J2EE environments

- Support for multiple industry-leading J2EE Application Servers and CORBA systems

- Provides an extensible framework for manipulating incoming and outgoing messages or to build custom dispatchers (e.g., integrate transactions, enterprise security, and compression algorithms)

- Runtime administration and control of running Web services via JMX

- Web based management console and management service

- Interoperability tested with over 15 SOAP implementations including Microsoft.NET and the Microsoft SOAP Toolkit

- Development portal www.xmlbus.com offers rich set of developer resources

*Source:* http://www.iona.com/products/webserv-xmlbus.htm. Used by Permission.

**Professional Services**   Besides earning revenue from the sale of its Orbix and other software environments, IONA makes money through the sale of services such as consulting and education.

On the consulting side, IONA provides expertise in assessing application environments, in providing architectural design services, and in the development and deployment of applications. Additionally, IONA has experience in application migration as well as CORBA application design experience.

On the educational side, IONA provides training on its own products as well as mentoring to help application developers learn how to build distributed applications. This kind of service will be extremely valuable as developers ramp up their Web services application development skills.

**Competitive Positioning**    IONA provides a distributed computing architecture that allows its customers to build e-business applications and that also has a consumer/business-to-business focus. The company fits into the Java "camp" along with IBM, Sun, et al.—but more closely resembles BEA, because not only does it make a Java application server software environment but it also sells professional services.

IONA and its direct competitors all base their business models on providing software and services. (Direct competitors include Silverstream, Lucin, Software AG, CapeClear, Velocigen, and Savvion.)

**IONA Summary**    IONA has a heritage of using standards to build distributed applications. The company has core expertise in such technologies as Microsoft's COM and the OSF's CORBA environments. So it's only natural that IONA pursue the development of distributed Web services applications using new Web services protocols and registries.

IONA's strategy is based on providing integration software for *e-business application environments*. In other words, the company has a specialty—business-to-business integration. Couple this with its knowledge of how to build distributed computing applications and its growing expertise in Web services, and IONA becomes a solid choice for business executives looking for Web services expertise that can help build business integration applications.

Note that IONA is much smaller than BEA and Microsoft, yet it can boast thousands of satisfied users. So the big question becomes, "How will IONA succeed against such large competitors over time?" By specializing in writing cross-platform, program-to-program Web services applications, IONA will be able to clearly differentiate itself from its much larger competitors. Thus it will be able to compete successfully against BEA's and Microsoft's respective Web services application server environments.

**webMethods Incorporated**

**Market Positioning**   webMethods is a leading provider of integration software that allows existing legacy, packaged, and/or custom applications to work together. The webMethods integration platform allows customers to achieve quantifiable R.O.I. by linking business processes, enterprise and legacy applications, databases and workflows both within and across enterprises. By deploying the webMethods integration platform, the company claims that its customers can:

- *Generate New Revenue Opportunities*—webMethods enables companies to increase market share by allowing them to bring products to market more rapidly.
- *Strengthen Relationships with Customers, Suppliers and Partners*—The webMethods platform provides companies the ability to interact directly and securely with a variety of customers, suppliers, and partners, resulting in streamlined business transactions and faster response times for customer inquiries.
- *Increase Supply-Chain Efficiencies*—webMethods solutions help companies achieve significant cost savings and productivity enhancements by reducing cycle times, lowering inventories, and reducing error rates through the real-time exchange of information.
- *Increase Returns on Technology Investments and Rapid Implementation*—The webMethods platform helps companies to maximize their return on investments in ERP and other enterprise applications by extending the benefits provided by those applications to a company's customers, suppliers, and other trading partners.

These four points echo several themes introduced earlier—namely, that Web services can help enterprises improve efficiency, reduce development costs, and create new revenue opportunities. In other words, WebMethod's strategy is synchronous with several of the ultimate aims of Web services.

webMethods has more than 750 customers worldwide, including Global 2000 leaders such as Citibank, Dell, East-man Chemical, The Ford Motor Company, Grainger, and Motorola. webMethods' strategic partners include Ariba, BroadVision, Cap Gemini Ernst & Young, Commerce One, Hewlett-Packard, i2 Technologies, J.D. Edwards, Microsoft, Oracle Corp., SAP AG, and Siebel Systems.

**Product Positioning**   The webMethods integration platform integrates application "adapters" with business process management software to help integrate core internal and external (with supply-chain business partners) information systems. The company has created adapters that enable applications from companies such as BMC Software, BroadVision, CommerceOne, Computer Associates, Hewlett-Packard Company, i2 Technologies, J.D. Edwards, PeopleSoft, and SAP to interoperate with one and other.

Worthy of note is webMethods' recent announcement that it can automatically Web services enable its adapters, so that existing applications can automatically communicate with each other using Web services WSDL and SOAP protocols.

Also worthy of note is the company's focus on management software that can allow an enterprise to manage business processes across the entire extended enterprise. The web-Methods integration platform provides an enterprise with a global view of its business, giving business executives immediate up-to-the-minute information from all of their systems and applications.

The company also has a growing professional services organization as well as many partnerships with much larger professional services firms, including Deloitte Consulting, EDS, KPMG Consulting, Accenture, and Lante.

**Competitive Positioning**   Dozens of software providers and professional services firms concentrate on providing products and services related to application integration. But this market generally segments into three sources of supply for such services:

1. Integration server providers.

2. Application server providers.
3. Professional services firms.

Integration server companies include suppliers such as webMethods, IONA, Tibco, and Vitrias. These companies focus specifically on application and data integration as well as integrated business process management. Additionally, a significant portion of their revenue stream may come from providing professional services related to the deployment of their products (in some cases, third-party professional services firms garner services revenue).

Application server providers include companies such as IBM, Microsoft, and Sun. These companies focus on providing application development environments (Java versus .NET and related middleware), integration services (each company offers application "connectors"), and business process management. Like integration server companies, these application server companies may offer professional services related to the deployment of their respective product suites.

The final source of supply for integration services is professional service suppliers such as GE Global Exchange Services or IBM Global Services. These companies may use their own application/integration server products (for instance, IBM Global Services has a heavy commitment to supporting IBM's WebSphere application server environment); they may have their own tools and methodologies (performing custom engagements using standard architectures such as EDI or CORBA combined with their own business process management software); or they may act as the deployment arm for any of a number of application server/integration server vendors.

From a comparative perspective, webMethods is positioned as an integration server vendor that focuses specifically on providing application/data integration and related professional services.

**webMethods Summary** webMethods has done an excellent job of adapting its adapters (program interfaces) to Web services, making it possible for existing packaged, custom, and legacy applications to automatically communicate with one another using Web services protocols. Further, webMethods focuses on providing management software, thus helping to fill in one of the shortcomings of Web services architecture—management. And webMethods does an excellent job of tying together business applications, Web services, and manageability with business process integration software, making the company an intriguing choice as a partner for enterprises looking to integrate existing solutions into a Web services architectural model.

## Category 2: Building Your Own la Carte, Point Product Web Services Applications

Up to now we have been discussing highly integrated Web services application servers. They have been hardware/software/services-based (from IBM, Sun, and HP), or they have been software-based (Microsoft) or software/services-based (BEA and IONA).

Businesses that buy these application server environments need to consider that they are paying a premium for the integration work performed by the provider. In other words, they pay for the work done by the vendor to integrate and quality-assure that the various software components work well together.

On the other hand, there are many point (individual) products that can be used to assemble Web services applications. A business using this point product approach does not end up paying a premium to a vendor for integration work. It is likely, however, that the business will end up doing some integration work itself (which has the effect of adding to the cost of a project anyway). So the business ends up doing a delicate balancing act—weighing the costs of buying a highly integrated (and expensive) complete application server environment against the costs of building one's own application server environment (and having to perform some application integration work between various point products).

This section describes some of the individual point products that can be used to build Web services applications.

**Example 1: Point Product Tools and Utilities**

There are literally hundreds of products that can be purchased to help build XML-based applications. These applications can then be made to communicate with other applications using Web services protocols and registries. The application development tools and utilities in the following list can be used to help build applications that use Java, C#, or other programming languages, which can then use Web services for program-to-program communications.

- Borland Delphi, C++ Builder, Progress Webspeed
- Oracle JBuilder, JDeveloper
- OpenROAD (Open Rapid Object Application Development)
- Magic eDeveloper
- Computer Associates' Jasmine
- Usoft's Bridge Server
- SAS Institute's SAS/Connect
- Compuware's Track Record
- IONA OrbixWeb for Java (we have seen that IONA provides a full application server environment, but it is also a provider of individual tools for point product application development)
- IBM offers a complete application server environment with WebSphere as well as individual tools for building Java-based applications with its WebSphere Studio programming products
- Macromedia's ColdFusion
- CodeWarrior for Linux
- Microsoft C-language development environments, plus Basic, Java, and other languages (like IBM and IONA, Microsoft makes full-fledged application server environments as well as language, business process management, and other point products)
- Sun Java (language, application server support)
- Oracle Java (language, application server support)

Forum
Systems

**Market Positioning**   Forum Systems is a great example of a point product solution that can be used in an a la carte manner to help build a Web services environment. As noted earlier in this book, security is a major concern with today's state-of-the-art Web services standards. Although security standards are evolving at the W3C, few enterprises are likely to use Web services to run mission-critical applications if security shortcomings are not addressed. This is where a point product solution such as the one offered by Forum Systems comes into play.

Forum Systems offers an XML "appliance" (a hardware/software combination) that is specifically designed to provide security for XML content sent over the Internet between business partners. The company contends that most of today's enterprise security solutions focus on securing *data in motion* over the Internet or through virtual private networks (VPNs). In other words, today's enterprises emphasize the purchase and installation of network firewalls, intrusion detection systems, and virus control software, and the use of data encryption techniques to secure data in flight.

Further, Forum Systems claims that few enterprises have taken the proper precautions to protect sensitive stored data (*data at rest*) either at the enterprise site or at their business partners' sites. And few have taken action to authenticate the sources of requests for data and content (as well as to structure authorization rights for certain users).

In short, for the most part, enterprise security measures have been designed to protect content and data at the network level and within certain containable domains. Forum Systems looks to use security standards and methodologies that protect content (documents, data, numbers stored in databases, transaction sets) that has been received via a network or stored on a local or business partner's remote server.

**Product Positioning**   Forum System's collaborative content security appliance enables enterprises looking to deploy Web services solutions to:

1. protect content *confidentiality*;
2. *authenticate* where content has originated and validate its origin and

3. provide only *authorized* users with access to certain types of content;

4. ensure the *integrity of data and content* that has been sent between communicating entities; and

5. provide *nonrepudiation* (a record that shows what transpired and who/what initiated it)

6. deploy *content-based routing* (a key technology in determining how content is handled based on enterprise policies). The identity of each transaction is detected and an intelligence layer can then be applied to determine how each transaction is secured, prioritized, and routed. The applications of content-based routing can be service-level agreements, quality of services, prioritizing transactions, and so on.

In other words, Forum Systems' appliance allows enterprises to protect content beyond the network level. It includes functionality to authenticate the sources of requests for data or content; to ensure data integrity, to provide nonrepudiation logging; and to handle the ever-increasing XML security checking and routing workload between collaborating enterprises (see Figure 10–1).

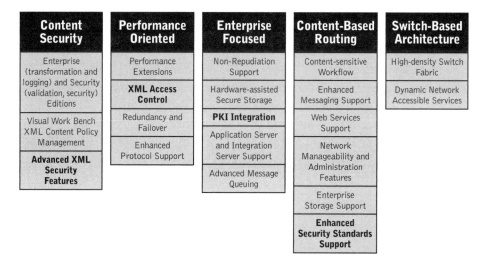

| Content Security | Performance Oriented | Enterprise Focused | Content-Based Routing | Switch-Based Architecture |
|---|---|---|---|---|
| Enterprise (transformation and logging) and Security (validation, security) Editions | Performance Extensions | Non-Repudiation Support | Content-sensitive Workflow | High-density Switch Fabric |
| Visual Work Bench XML Content Policy Management | **XML Access Control** | Hardware-assisted Secure Storage | Enhanced Messaging Support | Dynamic Network Accessible Services |
| **Advanced XML Security Features** | Redundancy and Failover | **PKI Integration** | Web Services Support | |
| | Enhanced Protocol Support | Application Server and Integration Server Support | Network Manageability and Administration Features | |
| | | Advanced Message Queuing | Enterprise Storage Support | |
| | | | **Enhanced Security Standards Support** | |

FIGURE 10-1    Forum System's Collaborative Content Security Architecture.
*Source:* Forum Systems, February 2002. Used by Permission.

In addition, an efficient collaborative content security system weighs the effect of adding these features and functions on the overall performance of existing networks and application servers. The Forum Systems appliance is positioned to help offload application servers from having to run additional security software as well as having to process and route thousands of XML files between various servers and applications.

**Competitive Positioning**     Should an enterprise wish to purchase security software that provides digital signature authentication, data integrity checking, content-based routing, et al., it is available from companies such as Entrust, RSA, IBM, Verisign, and many others. The disadvantage of this approach is that an enterprise would load this software on existing application servers, thus increasing their workload and potentially requiring a systems upgrade to handle increased security processing and content routing.

If, instead, an enterprise were to use an appliance approach, issues related to collaborative content security processing and increased workload processing would be offloaded from the server to the appliance—thus realizing certain performance benefits at the application server level. Forum Systems, and more recently McAfee and a few other companies, represent the first wave of vendors to bring such security appliances to market.

**Summary Observations**     As discussed earlier in this book, Web services standards must be enhanced to address shortcomings related to secure content handling. Without enhanced security, many enterprises will not use Web services-based applications in mission-critical situations. Forum Systems provides a solution to securing content in flight or at rest that can peacefully coexist in an Web services application environment. And Forum System's XML security appliance also is a great example of how Information Systems managers can use point product solutions to build their own Web services environments.

Example 2:
Using Open
Source to
Build Web
Services
Applications

We have discussed some of the many application development tools and utilities that can be used to build XML-based Web services applications. But where can the software that is needed (UDDI, SOAP, WSDL) be obtained? One example is an open-source Apache server.

**What is Open Source?**  Software that is open source is developed on a cooperative, collaborative basis by software developers worldwide. The resulting code is usually made available for public consumption as well as for use by organizations in commercially available products.

**How can you access Web services protocols through Apache?**  Start by going to www.apache.org. At this site you will find a listing of the various Apache projects underway, including the Apache XML project. This project contains various modules for XML application development and Web services application deployment.

In particular, within the Apache XML project is a module called the Apache SOAP project:

> The Apache Soap project is an implementation of the draft W3C protocol by the same name. It is based on, and supersedes, the IBM SOAP4J implementation.
>
> From the draft W3C specification: SOAP is a lightweight protocol for exchange of information in a decentralized, distributed environment. It is an XML based protocol that consists of three parts: an envelope that defines a framework for describing what is in a message and how to process it, a set of encoding rules for expressing instances of application-defined datatypes, and a convention for representing remote procedure calls and responses.
>
> *Source:* http://www.Apache.org. Used by Permission.

The code needed to build SOAP applications is readily available and free to download from this site. This approach represents another way to build Web services applications using the a la carte approach.

*Note:* Another open-source application server environment is offered by the W3C under the trademarked name "Jigsaw." Go to www.W3C.org for further details.

# Category 3: Web Services Professional Service Providers

Up to this point we've examined complete, turnkey Web services application servers, software-based application servers, and a la carte approaches to building Web services environments. These approaches work well those organizations that have development expertise available within, but for many small and mid-sized companies lack such expertise. In this section, then, we examine a few of the professional services firms that are planning to offer Web services application design and deployment services.

**GE Global Exchange Services**

**Market Positioning** GE Global eXchange Services (GXS) is part of GE Information Services, Inc., a wholly owned subsidiary of the General Electric Company. GXS operates one of the largest commerce networks in the world and has over 100,000 trading partners who participate on its electronic marketplace (doing over 1 billion transactions annually). To date the company has largely focused on EDI as a means to foster transactions between partners, but recently it has introduced XML and SOAP into its product offerings, signaling its move into Web services provisioning.

Like many professional services suppliers, GE Global eXchange Services not only provides consulting and development services but also builds software that it uses for systems integration purposes. Specifically, GXS builds various business integration tools and utilities that are used to help its customers integrate internal systems and/or integrate applications with external business partners. But the company's major focus is on working with its customers to "define, measure, analyze, improve, and control day-to-day business processes." First and foremost, GXS is a professional services firm.

The company focuses on four specific types of services (organized by division):

1. GE Integration Solutions—focuses on providing software and services that enable information sharing;

2. GE Interchange Solutions—focuses on providing software and services that enable companies to communi-

cate effectively and electronically with their business partners;

3. GE Marketplace Solutions—focuses on providing solutions related to the creation of public or private digital marketplaces.

4. Consulting Services—focuses on providing traditional consulting services such as needs assessment, business process consulting, and design and deployment services.

**Product Positioning**    Because GXS focuses strongly on supply chain and B2B electronic transactions, the company has many customers who make use of other program-to-program technologies to transfer transactional data between business partners. One of the first moves the company has made toward providing Web services for its customers has been to introduce an XML Schema that helps bridge different formats and communications methods (such as those used by Electronic Data Interchange—EDI).

The company's recently released XML Schema Plug-in helps developers save time converting data to/from XML. They can use it to automatically map transactions that are in a proprietary form (such as some data created using certain ERP or legacy business application environments) into XML schemas that help define the structure, content, and semantics of XML documents. As a result, data can be easily shared between existing and/or legacy application environments and newer Web-services-oriented distributed computing environments.

Other Web services protocols are starting to show up in various GSX products, such as the company's PetroDEX business exchange service that helps petroleum companies manage information associated with the shipment and delivery of gasoline and other refined petroleum products.

Here is an example of how GSX used SOAP to deliver a back-office program-to-program service for PetroDEX users:

GAITHERSBURG, Md., 09/18/2001—GE Global eXchange Services (NYSE: GE) today announced that it has added new capabilities to its PetroDEX data exchange for the U.S. Petroleum industry. The new capabilities include Web-based data management and back-office integration components that will enable petroleum companies to reduce costs and increase profitability through improved supply chain efficiency.

PetroDEX's new capabilities will help companies to simplify transactions, enhance customer service and automate labor-intensive processes. Available now, these capabilities include:

- Total ReconciliationSM—allowing companies to use the Web to more efficiently collaborate on the direct exchange of petroleum products, thereby reducing time-consuming error corrections and eliminating the need for costly in-house reconciliation systems.

- Chained Equity—since petroleum products often pass through several suppliers or marketers before reaching the final customer, this Web-based service enables refiners to reduce time to market by authorizing the entire chain of recipients in advance.

- Back-office integration—enabling the time-saving transfer of data directly to PetroDEX from enterprise systems using Internet protocols such as file transfer protocol (FTP) and simple object access protocol (SOAP).

"Having supported the petroleum industry with mission-critical data transactions for nearly three decades, PetroDEX now offer companies an even broader range of services for supply chain collaboration," said Harvey Seegers, president and CEO of GXS. "Through PetroDEX the petroleum industry now has a powerful new set of tools to manage information, increase efficiency and reduce costs."

*Source:* http://www.gegxs.com/gxs/press/release/09182001. Used by Permission.

**Competitive Positioning**    As a leader in providing the network, products, and services for B2B exchanges, GXS has few competitors that can scale to the over 1 billion transactions that the company now supports annually. And the company's recent business partnership with Commerce One (another large supplier of electronic marketplace services) further strengthens GXS' position.

However, GXS is not alone in providing large commerce marketplaces. IBM recently improved its position by partnering with Ariba and I2 and is now well positioned to compete with

GXS. (And IBM with its WebSphere product line has been far more aggressive about building Web services than GXS.)

**GSX Summary**   GSX is a fine example of a large professional services supplier that is moving toward Web services provisioning. The company has a large EDI base, and over 60% of its customers are Fortune 500 (large) companies. That customer base will need to adopt a Web services strategy over the next several years, and GSX is ideally positioned to provide the conversion systems from today's EDI commerce networks to Web services-based transactional systems of the future.

## Chapter Summary

This chapter has provided the background information you need to narrow your search for a Web services application development product suite or platform. Its aim is to steer you toward the best vendor with the best approach to meet your particular Web services application development needs.

In this chapter you learned that there are several ways to obtain Web services. First, you can buy a Web services application server environment (from either a hardware/software/services supplier or a software platform maker). Second, you can build one yourself, using a la carte programs or open-source software. Third, you can turn to a professional services supplier—GSX or IBM or any of a number of others.

If you look closely, you'll see that few vendors offer a comprehensive Web services development platform with full support for UDDI, WSDL, and SOAP. But vendors are building Web services applications today. They are doing it by mixing and matching existing applications environments (CORBA, for instance) with the Web services protocols that they do support. Remember, Web services applications can be built by using alternative programmatic interfaces to the WSDL and SOAP protocols and by hard-coding program locations as opposed to using UDDI. And this is what is happening today.

# 11

# A Review of Where This Book Has Taken Us

This book has addressed 10 questions that non-technical business executives would likely ask about Web services. The answers to these questions would help them understand the following:

- The definition of Web services.
- How Web services work.
- What the benefits of using Web services would be to their respective organizations.
- Who (what other accounts) are using Web services (and for what purpose).
- Where the "gotchas" are with this evolving new architecture.
- What the buying criteria and buying approaches are, should an organization wish to purchase the hardware, software, and/or services needed to build Web services solutions.
- Which vendors supply Web services solutions.

With this background business executives should now be prepared to make complex decisions like "when to deploy

Web services" or "which applications are candidates to become Web services applications."

## A Review of Each Major Part of the Book

This book has been organized into three parts: a *primer on Web services*, an *idea/strategic planning guide*, and *a buyer's guide*. This chapter summarizes the highlights of each part, chapter by chapter.

PART I:
A Web
Services
Primer

This part focused on "setting the stage." It defined what Web services are, how they work, and why previous attempts at providing such services have experienced limited acceptance. It also described shortcomings or "gotchas" related to state-of-the-art of Web services.

Definition

Chapter 1 presented a comprehensive view of the evolving Web services architecture.

From this author's perspective, the bottom-line simplest definition is that:

> Web services are a distributed computing architecture that relies on loosely coupled applications to facilitate cross-platform program-to-program communications. These applications can use similar or diverse development languages and platforms to communicate with each other over the Internet.

Chapter 1 focused not only on the various technical components that make up Web services, but also on the ancillary programs and products sometimes needed to build *complete* and robust Web services environments. Web services architecture can consist of just the products and programs needed to implement a simple message-based architecture (UDDI, WSDL, SOAP with XML content and Internet delivery) or of all of these protocols plus other software to improve business process flow, make application development easier, ensure reliability/availability/security, and the like.

**Program-to-Program Communications**

Chapter 2 explored how program-to-program communications work in order to offer business executives a better understanding of how programs can communicate with other programs over the Internet. It examined some of the previous program-to-program schemes of the past to show why they did not garner tremendous market acceptance. This review of Web services history gives you, as a business manager or IS executive, the background you need to defend a decision to strategically embrace Web services architecture.

This background should prepare you to: (1) handle objections that your company has "been here before" and (2) convince colleagues to get active in developing Web services applications for your company's strategic and competitive well-being.

This chapter also considered whether Web services are for real. For over 20 years, business executives and IS managers have heard vendors and standards organizations promise to make cross-platform program-to-program communications a reality—and yet a simple, elegant, backed-by-the-major-players approach never materialized. Today, however, Web services hold great promise of becoming the simple, elegant, universally backed program-to-program approach to cross-vendor, cross-platform communications that we have long been waiting for.

**How Web Services Work**

Chapter 3 reviewed how Web services actually work from a technical perspective. This chapter was designed for business executives who desire to understand the basic Web services technologies and associated acronyms in greater detail.

The most basic elements of a Web services architecture are (1) a common format, (2) a means for applications to "talk" with each other, and (3) a common network. XML, WSDL, and SOAP over an Internet network (using HTTP) enable these three things to happen. A UDDI registry is nice to have, but other work-arounds such as hard-coding the location of services applications can suffice when creating simple Web services application environments.

The big message to take away from this chapter is that, owing to certain immaturities in the overall readiness of Web services as an "enterprise-class" architecture, many early adopters are making use of other protocols or architectures to supplement Web services. For instance, if an enterprise wants to send XML transactional data to its business partners, in many cases that data will be sent using EDI or CORBA protocols in lieu of Web services protocols. And this will continue to be the case until Web services reliability, security, and scalability mature.

The same holds true for directory/registry services. Many applications today are actually "hard-coded" (their location will be known by the requester program, because it will be written into the requester program itself). Over time, as UDDI registries mature and proliferate, Web services applications will be able to automatically find each other. Until then, however, a lot of manual coding will be taking place to enable applications to find and bind with each other.

This chapter emphasized that using other protocols at this juncture is perfectly acceptable, given the comparative maturity of Web services versus the much stronger COM and CORBA programmatic interfaces and protocols. (The chapter also pointed out that these approaches were used because they were either expedient, preexisting, or cost-effective.)

## Limitations, Shortcomings, and Gotchas

All too often books on Web services overlook some of the shortcomings of today's state-of-the-art. In Chapter 4 you should have learned that Web services are great as a messaging architecture—but need improvements if they are to be used in enterprise-class, robust, reliable application environments. Amid all of the excitement and hype about Web services it is important to ground one's hopes and expectations for this architecture. Web services hold great promise—but they have quite a bit of maturing to do.

From a "great-promise perspective" Web services are expected to radically change the way that businesses can be structured and modeled. And, if properly designed and executed, Web services can help create additional business efficiencies, increase productivity, and provide new ways to bring products to market.

Also, note that most Web services shortcomings can be overcome using third-party hardware and/or software products. This is why this author believes that Web service can be used today in some mission-critical computing environments.

## What Does Web Services Enable My Organization to Do?

Chapter 5 illustrated some things that are possible to do with Web services. This chapter offered theoretical examples to help you think about applying some of these ideas within your own organization.

## Who Is Using Web Services: Real-World Examples

Chapter 6 is based on direct interviews with Web services users. And the research conducted to write this "real-world" chapter turned up some surprises. First, many early adopters were not using the whole Web services protocol and registry set to build their Web services applications. Second, no examples could be found to illustrate (a) how enterprises are using Web services to rapidly expand their existing applications portfolios, or (b) how enterprises are using Web services to create/overcome competitive pressure. The explanation seems to be that, at this juncture, Web services are not mature enough to warrant a complete redeployment of large enterprise application portfolios on a wide scale.

On the "pleasant surprise" side, the example of InterPro Partners was quite exciting. It showed InterPro using Web services protocols and registries not only to build Web services but also to create a radically new business model. (And this model gives InterPro very distinct advantages over its competition.)

Other examples were also exciting, but InterPro stood out because the company understood the importance of UDDI, was using Web services protocols, and was creating a whole new and competitive business model making use of new Web services technologies.

**When?**

Chapter 7 discussed "when" the appropriate time is to implement Web services.

To get started, business executives need to determine the technical competence of their own application development staff (particularly in the areas of object-oriented programming as well as in messaging architecture).

The next step is to find applications that your organization needs to implement—and then determine if Web services could serve as a viable architecture for their deployment.

To help illustrate when Web services should be used, this chapter asked, "Where are they being used now?" Enterprises are using Web services now for B2B transactions, for consolidating vast libraries of object code, to help reduce application development expenses, to open new markets, and for certain consumer "valet" services. If your organization has initiatives such as these, and Web services is a viable architecture for the purpose of developing new applications to suit these initiatives, the time to start building Web services applications is now.

**PART 3:
A Business
Executive's
Buyer's Guide**

The third part of this book focused on providing business decision makers with a description of the Web services/application server marketplace. It then examined products and services offered by many, randomly chosen vendors, focusing on market dynamics, architectures, competitive positioning, and related product offerings. The goal was not to declare "winners" and "losers," but to highlight the various approaches vendors are taking to bring Web services to market and then to review their respective product sets.

**Vendor
Selection
Criteria:
Three
Approaches**

In Chapter 8 you learned that there are three basic approaches you can use to build Web services:

1. *Buy a complete application server environment.* These come in two flavors: (a) a complete hardware, software, and services platform (from companies like IBM, Sun, and HP); and (b) a software (and sometimes services) approach that involves purchasing a complete application development environment that can be run on various hardware and operating systems environments

(from companies like BEA and Microsoft). (Note: Microsoft will someday make its .NET products available on Linux.)

2. *Buy a series of point products and build your own Web server environment.* This "a la carte approach" can be considerably less expensive but usually involves more integration work on the buyer's part in order to build sophisticated Web services applications. Also note that open-source Web services software can be obtained, serving to further lower the cost and expense of developing and deploying Web services applications.

3. *Buy professional services.* This approach advocates finding a professional services company that has expertise in Web services (a bit of a challenge at the time of this writing) and letting that company design, build, deploy, and possibly manage (outsource) your Web services applications. Though this approach does not quite have legs at present, expect Web services application development to be a high-growth area over time for professional services companies. (And the more professional services firms that participate, the more competition there will be—which should help lower your development costs.)

You should have walked away from this chapter with an understanding of your purchase options.

**J2EE versus .NET Market Dynamics**

Chapter 9 discussed the market schism between Java 2 Enterprise Edition (J2EE) and Microsoft .NET. Essentially, vendors have centered on two approaches to delivering Web services—a Java language-centered approach and a C# language approach manifest in Microsoft's .NET strategy. Vendors that have embraced the Java approach include Sun, Oracle, and IBM (and pretty much every other major player in the industry). Vendors that have embraced .NET include Microsoft and its many business partners. A few companies such as HP and Compaq do both.

The basic market belief is that the Java approach already offers cross-platform capabilities (because cross-platform code portability is central to Java's design goal), whereas Microsoft's .NET is focused on Intel platforms and has not been designed to promote code portability. This belief may or may not be true—but one of the key points in this chapter is: "It doesn't matter!" Why not? Because Web services enable applications to talk with other applications regardless of the platform on which the respective applications are running, and regardless of the application development language each application uses. So, to this author, the J2EE versus .NET discussion is a bit of a red herring.

Having said this, the chapter offers third-party Java opinion and a Microsoft response as to how the two approaches differ.

## Web Services Supplier Profiles

Chapter 10 explicitly set out to avoid declaring winners and losers in the Web services race. It is this author's basic belief that consumers of Web services win when there are many vendors that have rich Web services offerings—we don't win when one or two vendors lead the pack (because then there is no one to really interoperate with).

Having this as a goal, some vendors are further along in the sophistication of their product offerings and the level of integration between Web services development environments and ancillary software, such as business process management, personalization, and the like. This chapter presented individual vendor profiles that portrayed each vendor's market strategy, the status of each vendor's product set, and the respective competitive positioning—then concluded with a short summary evaluation of each vendor. No winners or losers were chosen....

# Summary Observations and Conclusions

**P**robably the biggest surprise for me in writing this book was the current state-of-the-art of Web services. Reports in the trade press, vendor hype, and even some customer testimonials led me to believe that Web services standards were more advanced and sophisticated than they really are. Web services have a lot of maturing to do in order to become viable for running mission-critical applications. Improvements need to be made in reliability, availability, security, manageability, routing, and numerous other areas in order to make Web services usable for large-scale secure transaction processing and other applications. But until the standard's mature, Web services can be augmented by third-party products and used in some mission-critical computing environments.

Another "shocker" was that Web services can be designed and delivered using XML and HTTP protocols—and without using UDDI, WSDL, and SOAP as middleware. Many companies interviewed and reviewed in the "real-world" chapter had made use of COM or CORBA middleware for program-to-program communications purposes, owing to certain shortcomings in Web services maturity. (Some of these shortcomings include reliability, security, and manageability.) In fairness, however, some of these companies had either in-house CORBA or COM expertise or existing COM or CORBA middleware that enabled them to deploy applications more quickly using existing people or existing code. So, for these companies, using non-Web-services protocols and registries proved more expedient.

Yet another surprise was the lack of use of UDDI registries. Most of the early adopters of Web services are not using UDDI registries—instead they are hard-coding (entering directly into their applications code) the addresses of the applications with which they want to cooperate. Still, at this juncture in Web services development, this practice makes good sense. You need a large number of applications to create a viable and useful public directory; and you need Web services applications to be reliable, secure, and robust in order to build a viable and useful private directory. The Web services applications architecture still needs to mature a bit in order to create viable enterprise-class solutions for public directories; and private Web services application modules need to be catalogued and quality-tested before being placed in a private UDDI registry.

On the positive surprise side I was very impressed with the level of cooperation that I saw between vendors. In the past, many vendors alleged that they were building a "standards-based" approach to cross-platform program-to-program communications—but often these same vendors made decisions that benefited themselves in the design of their respective architectures (alienating other vendors who were trying to follow their lead). And in the past, standards committees acted too slowly and produced standards that were far too complex (overorchestrated) and too cumbersome to be used by small- and medium-sized businesses. I was delighted to see the progress that has been made in building Web services. I am especially pleased to see the level of cross-vendor cooperation that is taking place between Microsoft and IBM in creating true cross-platform program-to-program communications using common Web service protocols and registries.

# Best Advice

The best advice this author can offer to business executives who are trying to figure out what to do about Web services is as follows:

1. If you make enterprise business-strategic decisions, it's time to become familiar with Web services. It is fairly straightforward to write and implement Web services applications—there are plenty of tools and utilities that can be used and there are some fairly comprehensive application server environments, such as IBM's WebSphere and Microsoft's Visual Studio .NET, that can enable you to easily write Web services applications. So get your feet wet—start to become familiar with Web services concepts and start to proto- type applications now.

2. Be aware that you have a year or two to become com- petent in Web services. Over the next few years, thanks to fast movement on creating standards by the W3C, many Web services shortcomings in the areas of reliability, security, manageability, and the like will be remedied. Expect that in two to three years Web ser- vices will start to proliferate (as UDDI public registries start to publish the availability of more and more Web services). At this point, be prepared to start shifting your application development efforts toward a Web services architecture—or risk your competition's doing so (and potentially disrupting your way of doing business).

If you are an individual, technically competent user, it is time for you to become familiar with Web services. New "agents" are coming to market that can do work for you and help improve your personal productivity. Start reading up on Microsoft's .NET strategy and its various Web services programs that can help you simplify message handling and calendar activities. And then use your imagination—start to look for new services coming to market that may be able to assist you in both your personal and business life.

Further, observe that your organization's initial experiments with Web services will likely fail if:

- The data that you seek to exploit cannot be put into a format and content architecture that enables you to share it with other applications;

- Applications can not be easily found and bound. Without being able to automate the process of finding and using Web services, application programmers will have to manually implement linkage to service applications in their code (defeating the automated/unattended aspect of Web services); and

- Your enterprise does not pay attention to how to flow Web services applications efficiently. Improper workflow and convoluted business processes make processing harder to do (thus defeating one of the key reasons for implementing Web services—to realize productivity and efficiency gains). As Web services start to proliferate, close attention needs to be paid to business process management and workflow in order to maximize potential efficiency gains that automated Web services can deliver.

## Parting Comments

Philosophically the move toward Web services makes a great deal of sense. As computer users we derive the greatest benefit from the *applications* that run on our computers—the internal software infrastructure and system design are only a means to an end (that end being to run applications).

Web services creates an environment that will enable developers to focus on building useful applications modules as opposed to building systems infrastructure. In days gone by we've seen many vendors invent and reinvent the same infrastructure components over and over again. (Infrastructure in this case refers to operating systems, middleware, communications/networking, systems management, and other elements needed to run a systems platform.) Think about it: how many versions of UNIX do we really need? And how many systems and network management packages do we really need? And how do we benefit from dozens of choices for network protocols? We don't benefit from reinvented infrastructure—we benefit from *applications!*

By being able to pick a Web service from column A and a complimentary Web service from column B (and so on), application developers will some day be able to choose from hundreds, thousands, and eventually millions of application modules in order to create applications on-the-fly. (In fact, application programming using Web services applications will become so easy that even nontechnical nonprogrammers will be able to design and build their own Web services applications, using simple native language commands and graphical user interfaces.) Accordingly, having access to more and more applications will be a huge win for users—we will gain access to more information services than ever before and benefit from personal productivity increases that result from this new generation of Web services applications.

Although I've expressed some reservations about the state-of-the-art of Web services today, I can clearly see the benefits that this architecture will bring to computer users in the near future—and I'm excited by it! I firmly believe that this time, because Web services are simple and straightforward to build and deploy, and because they have the strategic backing of every major vendor in the industry—we will finally see the cross-platform, program-to-program communications environment that we have so long desired come to pass.

# Index

*Page numbers in italics refer to illustrations.*

HALF PRICE BOOKS #00022
09/26/04 12:26

0000624049/TFH022/00001
CUSTOMER: 0000000000

1    @3.00      UC                    3.00
     5798-(Used books, clearance prices)
                                      12.98
1    @12.98     UN
     5799-(Used books at low prices)

                                       0.00
SHIP/HAND                             15.98
SUBTOTAL                               1.41
TAX (8.8% on $15.98)                  17.39
TOTAL

PAYMENT TYPE                          22.39
CASH                                  22.39
PAYMENT TOTAL           $
CHANGE DUE - CASH       $              5.00

              THANK YOU!

The perfect gift...HPB Gift Cards!
Choose any amount for any occasion


         END OF TRANSACTION

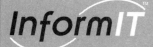

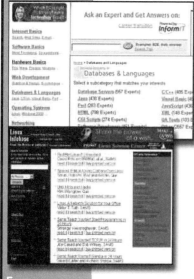

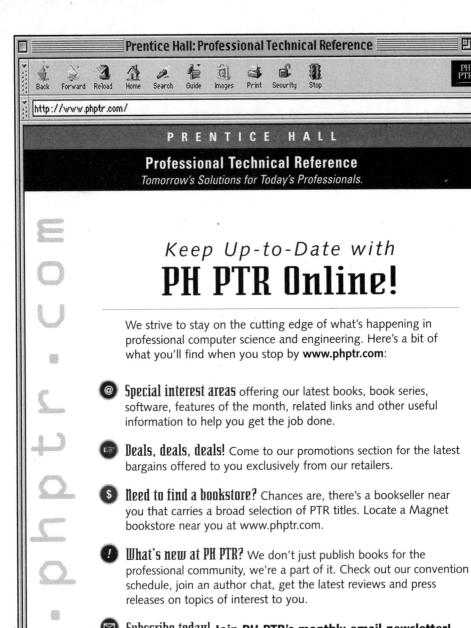